W9-BXX-656

Praise for
Bringing Heaven to Earth

"Oh, the difficulty of balance in this walk of faith. We tend to lose it. At least I do. I find myself on the side of the path, entangled in small issues and controversies. This book calls us to keep our eyes up. To keep the big things the big things. The authors offer a much needed and much welcomed reminder."
　　—MAX LUCADO, pastor and author

"For many Christians, heaven is just some place we fly away to. But Ross and Storment clear the clouds to reveal the ways in which heaven matters in the here and now. Earth is full of heaven, they say, but you have to know where to look and how to participate in it. Finally, a concept of heaven worth believing in!"
　　—JONATHAN MERRITT, author of *Jesus Is Better than You Imagined* and senior columnist for Religion News Service

"Christians need to get past all views of the future that do not impact the present. That is how Jonathan and Josh help us; they call us to a view of 'then' that matters 'now.' *Bringing Heaven to Earth* is a timely challenge to a church in need of a new way of telling time."
　　—RICK ATCHLEY, senior minister at The Hills Church of Christ, Fort Worth, Texas

"It's about time someone dismantled the view that Christianity and the church exist to be God's waiting room until we make it to heaven. Jonathan and Josh dismantle the fairy tale of heaven being a place of naked, winged babies playing harps on clouds. They replace that with the vision that Jesus and the New Testament both expect heaven to burst forth out of the church."
　　—TIM HARLOW, senior pastor of Parkview Christian Church, Chicago

"In *Bringing Heaven to Earth,* Storment and Ross show us that how we think of heaven truly matters only when we are able to see how it impacts the way we live, day in and day out. This book doesn't disappoint."
　　—COLT MCCOY, NFL quarterback and coauthor of *The Real Win* and *Growing Up Colt*

"For believers and nonbelievers alike, the idea of heaven often seems sentimental, escapist, and irrelevant. But in this powerful and inspiring book, Jonathan Storment and Josh Ross make heaven and earth collide. The good news is that heaven is a party already in full swing. So pull up a chair to the banquet table and be sure to bring a friend."

—RICHARD BECK, blogger, author, and professor of psychology at Abilene Christian University

"There is good news for those who feel they are done with church: God is not done with us! Josh Ross and Jonathan Storment marvelously describe a world to end all worlds—the world that is on its way. And they show how we are to live in the meantime. This book will revive your hope and electrify your imagination."

—IAN MORGAN CRON, best-selling author of *Chasing Francis: A Pilgrim's Tale*

"*Bringing Heaven to Earth* is proof that the Bible is extremely relevant in the past and present, and especially in our future. Reading this book will challenge you to look for opportunities to show God's love to everyone you encounter."

—BOB SMILEY, Christian comedian

"This cultural 'crash' between heaven and earth is so needed in a world that has been stuck between two extremes of trying to explain heaven away or making an escape to heaven through hopes of an early rapture. This life we live is just a rehearsal for the consummation of heaven uniting with earth one day. When we put works with our faith, we are giving our neighbors a taste of glory divine."

—STACY SPENCER, senior pastor at New Direction Christian Church, Memphis, Tennessee

"We live in a world that faces innumerable challenges, and the authors remind us that faith in Jesus gives us the power to be his holistic witnesses to the restoration and reconciliation work found only in Christ. You will be inspired and equipped by reading this book."

—DANIEL HILL, author of *10:10: Life to the Fullest* and senior pastor of River City Community Church, Chicago

"Jonathan and Josh will widen your view of heaven and the scope of God's mission on earth. This book will make your heart beat faster and your soul grow bigger for the things God cares about most."

—GENE APPEL, coauthor of *How to Change Your Church (without Killing It)*

Bringing
HEAVEN
to
EARTH

You Don't Have to Wait for Eternity
to Live the Good News

JOSH ROSS
and
JONATHAN
STORMENT

Foreword by Scot McKnight

WATERBROOK
PRESS

BRINGING HEAVEN TO EARTH
PUBLISHED BY WATERBROOK PRESS
12265 Oracle Boulevard, Suite 200
Colorado Springs, Colorado 80921

All Scripture quotations, unless otherwise indicated, are taken from the Holy Bible, New International Version®. NIV®. Copyright © 1973, 1978, 1984, 2011 by Biblica Inc.™ Used by permission of Zondervan. All rights reserved worldwide. www.zondervan.com. Scripture quotations marked (MSG) are taken from The Message by Eugene H. Peterson. Copyright © 1993, 1994, 1995, 1996, 2000, 2001, 2002. Used by permission of NavPress Publishing Group. All rights reserved.

Italics in Scripture quotations reflect the author's added emphasis.

Details in some anecdotes and stories have been changed to protect the identities of the persons involved.

Trade Paperback ISBN 978-1-60142-670-3
eBook ISBN 978-1-60142-671-0

Copyright © 2015 by Josh Ross and Jonathan Storment

Cover design by Mark D. Ford; cover photo by Tilby Vattard, plainpicture

All rights reserved. No part of this book may be reproduced or transmitted in any form or by any means, electronic or mechanical, including photocopying and recording, or by any information storage and retrieval system, without permission in writing from the publisher.

Published in the United States by WaterBrook Multnomah, an imprint of the Crown Publishing Group, a division of Penguin Random House LLC, New York.

WATERBROOK and its deer colophon are registered trademarks of Penguin Random House LLC.

Library of Congress Cataloging-in-Publication Data
Storment, Jonathan.
    Bringing heaven to earth : you don't have to wait for eternity to live the good news / Jonathan Storment and Josh Ross.—First Edition
        pages cm
    Includes bibliographical references.
    ISBN 978-1-60142-670-3—ISBN 978-1-60142-671-0 (electronic) 1. Heaven—Christianity.
2. Christian life. 3. Mission of the church. I. Title.
    BT846.3.S76 2015
    248.4—dc23

                                            2014049363

Printed in the United States of America
2015—First Edition

10 9 8 7 6 5 4 3 2 1

SPECIAL SALES
Most WaterBrook Multnomah books are available at special quantity discounts when purchased in bulk by corporations, organizations, and special-interest groups. Custom imprinting or excerpting can also be done to fit special needs. For information, please e-mail SpecialMarkets@ WaterBrookMultnomah.com or call 1-800-603-7051.

Contents

Foreword

There will be a first hour in heaven. Mind you, I don't know how long it will last and when it will happen. It might happen the moment we die, or the moment of the resurrection, or the first hour in heaven. But it will happen.

What will happen in that first hour in heaven? *All things will be made right.* That's precisely what heaven is.

All things means *all* things. Our relationship to God, to self, and to all others—parents, spouses, siblings, children, friends, neighbors, and community members—and to the world and cultures around us. Nations will be right with other nations. I'm looking at Americans who hate Arabs, at Protestant and evangelical Christians who raise their eyebrows about the Russian Orthodox or Italian Roman Catholics. All will be made right with one another.

The hour all things are made right is the hour we are reconciled, and for that to happen two other things have to happen in the first hour: we have to own up to what we have done with utter and eternal truthfulness, and we have to embrace the other with utter and eternal forgiveness. Yes, that too. All will be made right.

The task of Christians today is to live into that first hour. For some, that first hour is something to wait on. Recently, I was speaking at a church about heaven as a place where we will be reconciled with all others. A woman came up to me and said, "I have someone to forgive. But I'll wait until the first hour. It's too hard to think about now."

All will be made right in that first hour, but we are called, as Jonathan Storment and Josh Ross teach so well in this wonderful book, to bring heaven down—or to bring it from the future into the present.

Sad to say, some who will be in heaven will do their best to pout their way through that first hour. They'd rather heaven be more like now, where we can silence our way out of a relationship, or segregate ourselves from people of a different political view, theological persuasion, or ethnicity or cultural worldview. But heaven won't be like that because all things will be made right. All things, not just some things and some people. You and God and you and your spouse and you and your parents and you and all others you know.

Do you want to live into that kind of heaven? If so, this book is for you. *Bringing Heaven to Earth* aims to make those who believe in heaven take it so seriously they begin to live for it and in it now.

Scot McKnight

Professor of New Testament, Northern Seminary

Author, *The Heaven Promise*

Introduction

Good News for a Change

This is not another book that offers *Proof That Ninety Seconds in Heaven Is for Real*. Enough trees have been killed to make the point that sometimes people have near-death experiences. And sometimes they see things that would confuse even the writer of Revelation.

This isn't one of those books.

Strangely enough the Bible doesn't talk all that much about heaven or hell. Jesus rarely mentioned them, and much of what we think about the Age to Come is pure conjecture—aided by images from movies or writers of medieval fiction or dreams that people have after eating pizza late at night. Let's be honest: what happens after we die remains largely a mystery.

Rather than try to describe heaven in detail, this book looks closely at what heaven has to do with earth. The world we live in matters. And what we think about tomorrow impacts how we live today.

In his great book *The Skeletons in God's Closet,* Joshua Ryan Butler asks his readers to do a little experiment. Go to BibleGateway.com and search for the words "heaven and hell." If you do this, Butler points out, you will have zero search results. Because in the Scriptures there is not a single verse where heaven and hell appear together. Hell isn't heaven's counterpart.

This might shock you, considering the amount of times we've heard those two words in the same sentence. From preachers to bloggers to people standing on street corners with billboards. Most of us have just assumed that heaven and hell belong in the same category, but that's not the gospel story the Bible is telling.

But if you were to search Bible Gateway for "heaven and earth," you would have over two hundred results. Because hell isn't the counterpoint to heaven in the Bible—earth is. The two belong together. God made both heaven and earth; they are both current realities; and from Genesis to Revelation, the story is God bringing them back together.[1]

At the risk of being blunt, Christians have largely left behind the basic Christian story line in favor of something related to what the earliest Jesus-followers would have called heresy. Christians have misrepresented the gospel by emphasizing marginal themes at the expense of the central truths. The tragic result is that people have stopped thinking of the gospel as good news.

We wrote *Bringing Heaven to Earth* because we are Christians who are concerned about the church's witness. Many Christians care a lot about saving people's souls. We care about that too. Yet what we observe is that they want to introduce more people to Jesus, but they find themselves at a loss when it comes to living a robust life of discipleship. We don't believe the primary purpose of following Jesus is to enjoy the gift of heaven. Rather, it is to be united with Christ in His love and mission. The call to conversion in the New Testament isn't a decision for salvation, but a decision for Jesus. It is more than a change in status; it is a shift in allegiance, passion, and calling.

Some Christians care a lot about justice and mercy ministries. They want to change the world by serving the "least of these" but often find themselves angry at those who don't see things the way they do. There are a lot of people who set out to save the world—for a few months or even years—but oftentimes they eventually grow bitter and weary. We think they need a bigger, and *far better,* story to enter into.

Jesus taught us to pray for His Kingdom to come right here on earth as it is in heaven. Both of us pastor churches filled with eager, sincere, committed Christian people. One of the congregations is in a college town, Abilene, Texas, and we find that young-adult Christians are looking for ways to follow Jesus that make a difference in the here and now.

The other congregation worships and serves in a transient, multicultural community in Memphis, Tennessee. We don't have to hunt around to uncover injustice, suffering, and great need. The struggles that people face are evident. The question is this: What is a Christian's responsibility to bring to bear God's will in this corner of the world, so that people throughout Memphis might come to experience a hint of what life is like in heaven?

We wrote this book because, in our experience, Christians are the best reason for someone to follow or not to follow Jesus. And right now, at least in the Western world, it seems like the evidence for the latter is stacking up. How many Christians do you observe and then think: *I want to be like them*?

They are said to follow the Prince of Peace, so why do Christians have a knack for coming across as divisive, anxious, fearful, and angry? For people who follow a Man who kick-started His ministry with a wedding party that rivaled Woodstock, Christians often are perceived as resentful, sour, and against anything that might resemble a celebration. For a group of people who follow a God who entered the world in the flesh, we often seem like we can't wait to escape this world.

We realize we are painting with a broad brush, and this may not be your experience. But from people who are on the outside of the Christian faith looking in, these are the observations we hear most often.

"Christians are too heavenly minded to be of any earthly good." I'm sure you've heard that saying. But what if the problem isn't that we've thought too much about heaven, but that our thinking about heaven is too separate from our life on earth?

When the topic of heaven comes up, too often it focuses on who's in and who's out. That is not what this book is about. We wrote *Bringing Heaven to Earth* because we believe there are core tenets of the gospel that have been lost in Western Christianity. While that has resulted in many people feeling that the gospel is no longer good news, they wish it still was.

We believe that in the end, God is not going to let Satan and his friends win anything. We wrote this book because we believe the clock is ticking on injustice, and we are convinced that it's time for some good news *for a change.*

And we wrote this book because we believe that the real good news leads to all kinds of change in this world.

Part 1

A Reintroduction to Heaven

We often miss the link between the beginning of Genesis, the creation account, and the closing of Revelation, a picture of the new heaven and the new earth. If you read these accounts together, it's almost as if the first book of the Bible and the last are in conversation with each other.

Revelation calls to mind the Garden of Eden, then tells us: "No longer will there be any curse" (22:3). With all of our being we want this to be true, but it's hard to grasp. No one on earth has lived in creation that is not tainted by a curse. All we know is a world in which we age, our bodies wear out, people die, and the Yankees and Red Sox get all the attention every summer.

God wants to reacquaint us with His creation as it was at the start. The garden one day will be restored. God will reverse the curse.

I don't know anyone who would not welcome this. Still, life in heaven seems distant. And the prevailing belief is that we will have to die before we can experience freedom from the curse of the garden.

But Jesus saw things differently. When He spoke about the Kingdom of God—and He spoke about it a lot—He was talking about the way His followers could bring heaven to earth. "Your kingdom come, your will be done, on earth as it is heaven" (Matthew 6:10).

Assuming Jesus was intentional about the words He included in the model prayer—and we both do—then the life of heaven can somehow be brought to earth. Not at the end of time when God comes to set things right, but today, in everyday life. Even in the midst of suffering and violence and poverty, God's Kingdom can reveal the life of God to those of us who live on earth.

We can introduce aspects of heaven to people in our cities, communities, neighborhoods, families, and circle of friends. Let's take a look at how that can be done.

When Heaven Comes Home

Jesus Taught Us to Pray for
Heaven-Earth Collisions

> Peter went inside and found a large gathering
> of people. He said to them: "You are well
> aware that it is against our law for a Jew to
> associate with or visit a Gentile. But God has
> shown me that I should not call anyone
> impure or unclean."
>
> —Acts 10:27–28

(Josh) was finishing preparation for a Christmas sermon when I heard the tragic news that a young man had opened fire on school children in Newtown, Connecticut. Twenty-seven people died, including the killer. Feeling numb and confused, I tried to finish what I had planned to say about Jesus's coming into this world to make things right. I needed the hope of Jesus's first arrival to once again nurture and tend to my heart.

Another time when I was writing—completing work on this chapter, in fact—I heard more disturbing news. ISIS was on the move, Ebola was striking fear in human hearts, and no matter how you interpreted the events in Ferguson, Missouri, something had gone badly wrong.

Sometimes I feel like hope is dangling on a piece of thread, but at least it dangles. It has not been severed. And sometimes, I don't need a burning light; I just need a ray of hope. A simple reminder that Jesus has won—*and will* win.

There are days when it looks to us as if evil is winning and running up the score. I'm not sure what to make of it. And what should our response be? Should we take our children out of public schools? Remove ourselves from public places? Give in to fear? Many choose some or all of these options as a means of escape.

But Jesus didn't escape risk. One of the best meals He served took place in an open field where thousands of hungry people had gathered. Jesus fed them. All of them. And before the food was served, He healed the sick who were there. Some of the people who sat down to this all-you-can-eat buffet were enjoying their first meal without chronic pain, nagging arthritis, and other ailments. These weren't just people who were eating; they were restored people.

Did you know this is the only miracle that is recorded in all four Gospels? It often escapes our notice that just before Jesus carried out these acts of healing and then feeding the masses, He found out that John the Baptist, His relative, had been beheaded. "When Jesus heard what had happened [to John], he withdrew by boat privately to a solitary place" (Matthew 14:13). Driven by grief, Jesus was looking for solitude. Yet, as He wiped tears from His eyes, He could see people coming from a distance. Thousands of people were coming toward Him.

The miracle that is described four times in Scripture was born from a moment of mourning. Jesus knew that even in the midst of tragedy, heaven falls to earth. God's life collides with the broken parts of earthly life that need to be restored.

Jesus taught us to pray prayers of engagement. He instructed, commanded, and commissioned His disciples to march into arenas of injustice and to lavish those spaces with love. When Jesus taught us to pray for God's will to be done—and for God's Kingdom to come—to "earth as it is in heaven," He taught us to pray for collisions (Matthew 6:10). Jesus has told us to pray that heaven will merge with earth.

WHEN WORLDS COLLIDE

Paul Haggis is a Hollywood director, producer, and screenwriter. After cutting his teeth writing for television shows such as *Diff'rent Strokes* and *The Facts of Life,* he helped create a number of television series. The most notable for me, as a born-and-raised Texan, was *Walker, Texas Ranger.*

Paul and I have never met, but in 2005 we both celebrated some great accomplishments. My buddy Kevin and I won the World Series in MLB 2005 on Xbox, and Paul won two Oscars. Okay, so his achievement may have been a little bigger than mine. Paul Haggis was honored for his work in two films he wrote. In fact, he became the first individual to have written two Best Picture Oscar winners in consecutive years.

Even if you aren't a movie fan, you probably have heard of both of these award-winning films. One is *Million Dollar Baby.* The other was based on the Hollywood producer's personal experience. In 1991, Haggis's Porsche was carjacked outside a store in Los Angeles. Though he wasn't in the car when it was stolen, it was an event that wouldn't leave him. More than ten years after losing his Porsche, Haggis would write one of the most creative, raw movies of the last decade. For the title he settled on one word: *Crash.*

This is not a movie you'll want to watch with your family around the Christmas tree next to a fire while eating gingerbre

It's rated R for good reason. There are sexually explicit, violent, intense, and suspenseful scenes. But the genius of the movie is that it tackles twenty-first-century racism in a way that doesn't make any one race, nationality, or social class the hero. Every group has noble traits and glaring flaws. And the characters in the movie who were born on third base and thought they had hit a triple are challenged to the core to redefine what it means to be human.

The movie begins and ends with automobile collisions. They are minor fender benders, but there is meaning in each one: the only way some people come into contact with others who are unlike them is to literally experience a crash. A collision. An unexpected encounter. An unplanned relational appointment. That makes this movie rich in meaning and insight.

A Good Story Brings Us Together

Beginning with Jesus's birth, the New Testament is jam-packed with heaven-earth collisions. Through Jesus, heaven came to permeate earth. You don't catch images of God strapping devices on the backs of humans to transport them out of the world and into space. Instead, you are bombarded with images and stories of heaven colliding with earth.

When Jesus was born, news of His birth reached the ears of shepherds, astrologers, and religious figures. The news also reached King Herod, and it's an understatement to say he was troubled. Angels kept showing up saying things like "Don't be afraid." But think of Mary. Of course she was afraid! Being greeted by an angel had never been part of her morning routine.

Angels announced a collision, and it was made known to the rest of us with the arrival of Jesus. Ever since, heaven has been invading earth.

Mary and Joseph received a baby blessing from Simeon when they presented Jesus in the Temple. The blessing doubled as a prophecy: "This child is destined to cause the falling and rising of many in Israel, and to be a sign that will be spoken against" (Luke 2:34). What kind of baby blessing is that? This tiny infant was to be a sign that would be opposed?

No one would have blamed Mary if she had responded, "Well, thank you," then turned to Joseph and whispered, "I told you we should have been blessed by the priest at the Third Synagogue instead of here." But Simeon knew something that most of the world didn't: heaven was coming to make earth right.

MOVING INTO THE NEIGHBORHOOD

Kayci and I (Josh) moved into the Binghampton community of Memphis in the summer of 2011. It's a neighborhood with rich diversity and culture. And for the first few weeks after we moved there, I took Mondays off as a family day.

One Monday afternoon in the fall, after I had just come in from playing baseball with my two boys, I noticed two police officers walking through my yard. They both had hands on their guns. I moved to open the door to ask what was going on. One of the officers raised his hand, telling me to stay inside. I told Kayci to take the boys to their room and to play on the floor. I reached for Truitt's Dallas Cowboy helmet. (Truitt was five at the time.) I was ready to go to war. Then I thought about how disappointing the Cowboys had been playing and decided it wouldn't help much.

I watched as the officers jumped fences, looked behind sheds, and crept around houses. I felt as if I was in the middle of an episode of *LAPD*.

Come to find out, there's a neighbor not too far from my home who has a boyfriend who beats her. She'll call the cops, and then when they show up to arrest the man, she decides not to press charges. After kicking him out of the house for a few days, she lets him back in. Then he beats her again, and the cycle is repeated.

She sat on her front porch with a bleeding face. I wanted to grab her by the shoulders and ask her, "Do you not know that you were created for more than this? You don't have to take it! You were made in the image of God. He adores you. Don't you know that?"

Maybe this neighbor needs God to visit her in a dream like He did Joseph (see Matthew 1:18–25). Or maybe she needs a God-given friend who can speak life into her soul. We know she needs a God-appointed collision. With some things in life, it takes a collision to make you stop and ask what really matters. A place where an unexpected encounter gives birth to a friendship that transcends superficial talk. Such collisions can lead to the healing of a broken heart.

THERE AREN'T ENOUGH CHAIRS? GET A BIGGER TABLE

Peter, who is known as an outspoken disciple of Jesus, had a collision with a man named Cornelius. The two were not friends. In fact, Peter and Cornelius couldn't be friends. This is why the story told in Acts 10 would make a great Broadway show.

Peter was a devout Jew. Even though he had seen Jesus cross racial lines to extend compassion, he still found himself immersed in Jewish tradition and custom. Jews were careful about what they ate and with whom they associated. Cornelius, on the other hand, was a Gentile and a Roman. Even worse, he was a Roman army officer. But he prayed to God regularly, he gave to the poor, and he feared God.

Try to find fault with that résumé. Still, Peter could not associate with this Gentile. They would never sit at the same table at a banquet. They would never shoot a game of pool together. Since Peter was a Jew, he knew who was in and who was out. Cornelius was an outsider. He ate forbidden things, like pork ribs and seafood gumbo.

But the beauty of this story is found in the collision. Two lives collided because of the main Character in the tale—God. A vision came first to Cornelius, the Gentile, and then to Peter. By now it shouldn't surprise us that God visited the outsider first. Following the dream, the servants of Cornelius went to Peter, and Peter gave them lodging. Think about that. If Peter's Jewish friends found out Gentiles had been invited to sleep under his roof, there would be some explaining to do.

Later, Peter met Cornelius and the impossible happened. The Roman soldier, enemy of the Jewish people and a Gentile at that, invited Peter to stay for several days. Peter stayed with Gentiles, slept in their home, ate with them. His Jerusalem buddies would have a fit when they found out.

Here's what often is missed in the story: Cornelius *and* Peter get converted. Cornelius is converted to Jesus. For Peter, it's not that he's converted and saved, but he definitely experiences a deeper conversion into the mission of Jesus. A Jew and a Gentile, both believers, became part of the same community: the family of God. They both enlisted in the same movement: the Jesus Way.

This should have been nothing new to Peter. Jesus taught him to pray for collisions such as this one. When Jesus taught His disciples to pray, He didn't ask God to snatch His people from this world. It was just the opposite. Jesus prayed for the behavior of heaven to invade the space we occupy right now. We are told to ask God to infuse the earth with His power, values, and principles.

Two thousand years later, on another continent and in a very different time and culture, a man named Oshea Israel got out of prison. Upon his release, a woman named Mary Johnson threw a surprise party. Together with some nuns she had gathered, they welcomed Oshea back into society. The party was a way to welcome him home.

Oshea had been locked in prison for years for second-degree murder. When he was a teenager he had gotten into a fight with a young man named Laramiun Byrd and had killed him. Now Oshea was thirty-four and starting over, and Mary Johnson thought this was something worth celebrating.

The twist in the story is that the man whom Oshea had killed was Mary's son, her only child. After Oshea was convicted, Mary knew she couldn't forgive a killer. But she realized she might be able to forgive a person.

She went to visit Oshea in prison. She recalled her conversation with him: "I just told you [Oshea] that I didn't know you; you didn't know me. . . . But we needed to get to know each other."

Oshea said later that this encounter was painful because Mary Johnson's son became human to him. As their initial meeting came to a close, Mary found herself surprised by what she did. She gave Oshea a hug. Now, years later, she still has not let go.

When he was released from prison, Mary asked Oshea to move in next door to her. He accepted. She says since her natural son is dead, Oshea will be her spiritual son.[1]

Only God can do something like that.

CHRISTMAS IN CONNECTICUT

Around the time of the tragedy in Newtown, Connecticut, I (Josh) sat in my office early on a Sunday morning, preparing to preach the first of three sermons in a series called Adventure. The message was a simple one: Immanuel, God with us.

Like most Sunday mornings, I got to the church office before 6 a.m. For some reason, as I prayed and looked over my notes, I was in a funk.

It wasn't the feeling of being under the weather. It was deeper than that—something was disturbing my heart. But I couldn't put my finger on it.

At 7:45 I texted Kayci. We usually chat on Sunday mornings right about that time. I asked her to pray for me because something didn't feel right. She said she would, but she also dug deeper. I'm grateful to have a wife who is sensitive to the Lord. If she believes she has a word from God, she doesn't hesitate to speak it.

She prodded with this question: "Do you think there's something you're about to say in your message that God may not want you to say? Pray through your notes again."

I studied my notes and it hit me. I didn't hear the audible voice of God, but there was clarity in my heart. It wasn't that I was about to speak a word that wasn't pleasing to God's heart. It was something else. The word was this: *You are about to preach a message about Immanuel—with us is God. I need you to believe this message more in your heart.*

I need the message of the abiding presence of God to carry me through life in deeper ways. Though I sometimes run from or ignore the abiding presence of God, He continues to hunt me down, to find me, and to work His will in my life.

The "God with us" promise needs to be rekindled in my heart, and in yours.

PACKING TAMBOURINES

God's people in the book of Exodus had been stripped of dignity, hope, and humanity. They were slaves nearly twice as long as the United States has been a nation. The "God with us" promise was hanging by a thread. As the Israelites prepared to leave Egypt, Scripture tells us they plundered the Egyptians. But seriously, how many possessions could you carry when you were setting off on foot, first to cross a sea and then to cross a wilderness?

After they crossed the Red Sea, we are told about their first possession. It wasn't something practical like a frying pan, a shovel, or a bow and arrow. It was a tambourine.

Of all the items they could have packed for the long trip, many of the Israelites made sure to bring musical instruments. We can assume they were preparing for a big party. They didn't know how the story would unfold, but they believed God was going to do something worth celebrating.

The "God with us" promise was rekindled in their hearts, and they began to dance and sing. How could anyone remain still after God had delivered His people in such dramatic, miraculous fashion?

The early Jesus-followers got this. Sure, they got distracted with keeping laws and abusing spiritual gifts, as well as the daily struggle of pledging allegiance to Jesus and not to Rome. But when they were at their best, they lived from the conviction that God had done something worth celebrating, and that the celebrations would continue.

The Temple stood in Jerusalem, a place where people went to worship and to get a picture of God's dream for the world. The early followers of Jesus were taught that they were mini-Temples of the living God. They didn't go to the Temple to meet with God, but they lived as people who were inhabited by God. They didn't take lessons *about* God into the world; they *took God* into the world. Or better said, God went with them. Immanuel, God with us.

Fifty years after D-Day—the Allied invasion to push the German army out of France—two survivors told their stories of what it was like that day. Troops crossed the English Channel and landed on the beaches of Normandy. The Germans had the high ground and were firing down on the Allied forces. One of the men said that as he approached the beach landing, he thought to himself, *There is absolutely no way we are going to win this war.*

The other man was a pilot who was in the air that day. He said when he looked down and saw what was about to take place, he thought to himself, *There is absolutely no way we are going to lose this fight.*

Sometimes what we need is perspective. We need God to give us a glimpse of what is to come so we can begin to live in His restored future now.

In Jesus, we learn that God comes with all His gifts, power, and presence. The Immanuel story tells us that senseless shootings in elementary schools, movie theaters, and shopping malls won't have the last word. Neither will ALS, cancer, heart disease, leukemia, or famine.

This is the story that compels us to pray for the people in our world who plot violence, that God will raise up His church to seek out the angry and confused and to lavish them with unconditional grace. We need to extend compassion in acts of service and care before great tragedies happen, as well as afterward.

God is on the move on earth. For two thousand years, God's people have come together on Sundays to worship. But when the followers of Jesus are at our best, we know that God's people don't stay in church. Saints know when it's time to leave home. God is on the move, and we are with Him. Let's join in the restoration of the world.

Let's march.

When the Saints Go Marching ~~In~~ Out

Are We Called to Retreat or to Engage Life in the Here and Now?

> There is no school to learn how to love your
> neighbor; just the house next door.
>
> — Bob Goff

I f you have entered into a covenant with Jesus, your home is more than a house number followed by a street name. It is a mission for the Kingdom of God.

Our culture has confused our role in the world. The home is said to be a place of refuge, a place where we escape to enjoy leisure and catch up on television programs. Not all of that is bad. But your home is much more than a place of safety and rest. For a follower of Jesus, the home is also a place where mercy, love, and grace flow for the benefit of others. Kingdom-people exist to bring neighborhoods and communities to life.

After living in our neighborhood for more than a year, I (Josh) found myself not being as intentional a neighbor as I should be. There are times when Jesus is the closest companion you could ever want, and there are other days when He comes across as a nagging nuisance.

Jesus has been described as the Gentle Healer and the Hound of Heaven. He keeps going after the same heart that He so carefully tends to. Have you ever felt annoyed by Jesus's persistence? I have.

One Wednesday night in December, I had a lengthy prayer time with the Lord. I was alone at our church facility, and I talked to God about needing to take to heart Jesus's words concerning loving my neighbors. I asked God to give me opportunities and to give me boldness and courage to act on this command. To be honest, I've been known to run in the other direction when doors are opened because I don't have the time, energy, or want-to. At times, I've made a pretty good priest and Levite in the good Samaritan story in Luke 10. It is like I see a person who is bloodied and abandoned at the side of a road, and I just keep heading to my destination.

That night after prayer, I pulled into my driveway about 8:30, and a neighbor across the street came running over. She was waving her hands in the air and screaming for help. I didn't know if someone had been shot, if her home had been broken into, or if someone needed medical attention. Then my neighbor uttered words that would make anybody squirm: "There is a mouse in my sink. Can you help?"

This friend had grown up in a Memphis neighborhood called Orange Mound—which is a tough place. She could probably have taken me out with her flip-flop. (Even in my neighborhood I have seen some women fight, and I have concluded they could hold their own in a cage fight.) But when it came to a mouse, this neighbor didn't want anything to do with it.

And neither did I. Seminary and more than a decade of experience as a pastor hadn't prepared me for rodent extermination. So I did what most humans would do: I tried to think of a good excuse. All I could think of was stuff like "My wife asked me to do the dishes" or "I'm allergic to mice." Neither seemed like a viable option.

Then it hit me. I had just spent more than an hour laboring before the Lord in prayer about loving my neighbors. Maybe this was a small way to enter more deeply into Jesus's invitation.

"Ma'am, give me a moment, okay? Let me think of a strategy." Without missing a beat she said, "Boy, we ain't got no time for no strategy. Get in there, and get the mouse!"

I didn't hesitate. I walked into her kitchen to see a mouse about the size of a half dollar. I could see the rodent was afraid, and I began to think through options:

- Option 1: Flush it down the garbage disposal. Don't judge me. Half of you think that was a brilliant idea. But the garbage disposal was on the other side of the sink partition.
- Option 2: Set a mousetrap, put it in the sink, go to the other room, and wait for the snap. Quick. Easy. Not much trouble.
- Option 3: Attempt to safely transport the mouse from the sink to a place outside where it could run free.

I wish I could say it was out of the goodness of my heart that I chose Option 3, but it was actually the most time-efficient plan I had. I put on an oven mitt and scooped up that bad boy, then he immediately ran up my arm. I admit that at that moment I screamed. Then I put an oven mitt on my other hand, cupped the mouse, ran outside, and set it free.

That night I was known as the hero of the neighborhood.

PRESSING INTO THE WORLD

Sometimes we march into unexpected places to do something as strange as helping to get a mouse out of a neighbor's sink. Other days we may be asked to march into someone's relational dysfunction, broken home, emotional crisis, or financial struggle. Each week greets us with moments to march into places of injustice and extreme forms of pain, sometimes to heal and cure it; other times to simply be present in the mess.

But we march. We don't march away from people and into the safety of our homes. We march toward people and their needs. When we march into relationships and situations where love and restoration are needed, heaven begins to shrink the distance between despair and a richer life.

This goes beyond working up enough courage to enter into someone's time of need. It gets at how we interpret Scripture. When we read the Bible, do we see the world as something to *retreat from* or to *run into*? So much hinges on whether we prioritize escaping or engaging.

If the world is essentially a trash heap that God is eager to set on fire, then we will regard it as having little or no value. We won't have second thoughts about retreating from the world. But if we read God's Word and see that the world is something to be cared for, nurtured, and brought to life, then we will approach people and the rest of creation as being in need of redemption and complete restoration.

A DIFFERENT WAY TO MARCH

For many of us, Ephesians ranks among our favorite books of the Bible. It is a frequently read book, but a basic point about Ephesians often is missed: it is a letter written to people living in Ephesus.[1]

Some history is in order. The church in Ephesus began with twelve people (see Acts 19:1–7). Then Paul showed up and began speaking in the synagogue, but they weren't buying what he was selling. So he went across the street to the hall of Tyrannus (see verse 9). His attitude was, "If you don't want me talking about Jesus on 'religious space,' I'll take the message to 'secular space.'" For Paul, sharing Jesus to the world wasn't about enjoying home-field advantage. He gave that up after his conversion.

Then miracles broke out, and there were some crazy ones. Televangelists now use handkerchiefs and aprons to exploit people, promising that these items have healing power—if you'll first send in twenty dollars. But in Ephesus, handkerchiefs were used to heal the sick. In a city known for magic, new believers began burning their magic books. Some may object that the converts in Ephesus could have been better stewards by selling the books for a profit, but unfortunately Amazon and eBay didn't exist yet. Their attitude was that if they were going to bury their past by dying to it, the books needed to die as well. They burned piles of books. (Harry Potter would be ticked!)

Ephesus was a city of roughly 250,000 people. It would rank as the seventieth largest city in the United States today. It was the center of the world for witchcraft, which is one reason Paul talked more about spiritual warfare here than in any other letter he wrote. Most residents of the city followed the teachings of a cult, believing their deity would grant them power and prosperity.

The city was home to more than twenty pagan temples. And it was arguably the most sexualized city the world knew at that time. Every spring, one million people would travel to the temple of Artemis, which had hundreds of temple prostitutes. It was considered worship to engage in intercourse with them. The people of ancient Ephesus believed such acts pleased the gods. Last but not least, Ephesus was home to the Festival of Dionysus, the world's largest keg party.[2]

This city presented all kinds of challenges to Jesus-followers. The powers of darkness had so many tools at their disposal. They could appeal to every human weakness. They had visible methods of luring people. They had effective strategies to captivate the mind, heart, intentions, and allegiances of people living in Ephesus and those who visited the city.

If you and your family had surrendered your lives to Jesus, you could easily make a list of reasons to leave Ephesus. In this city more than any other, the option of Christian flight seemed right. But not even once did Paul tell Jesus-followers to leave Ephesus. There is no hint of "If you're serious about Jesus, you will leave this polluted place. Think about your children and protect your family from all the immorality!" Instead, he assumed the new believers would remain in Ephesus. Consider the fact that the most evil, most immoral cities of the first century were immortalized, in part, when books of the New Testament were named after them. God didn't give up on the people . . . or the cities they lived in. And neither did God's church.

Paul's main goal was to equip Christians in Ephesus to live for Jesus in the middle of celebrated evil. He taught that we are equipped for an upside-down kingdom. We are equipped to stay, invest, and be the change. We are to be God's Kingdom in the world.

It makes sense, then, that Paul's letter ends with a description of the armor of God, not instructions for fleeing to a safer, more righteous place. And the crazy Jesus-followers took him seriously. They stayed in Ephesus and began to march. Once they had marched into evil, but now they marched for the Kingdom cause. They once celebrated evil. Now, they celebrated differently and resurrection broke in.

A NEW KIND OF HEAVEN AND A NEW KIND OF HERO

Sometimes we think of heaven as a one-way street, that Jesus came to earth, did His thing, and then went away. And now, blessings from heaven are here, but the road between earth and heaven still goes only one way. The things of earth follow the road of Jesus's ascension. People go to heaven. But the road from heaven doesn't flow to earth like it once did. We eventually go *there,* but *there* doesn't come here.

That is a common view, but what if it's not an accurate understanding of the relationship between heaven and earth? What if heaven is *here*? Not here simply to get us to the afterlife, but to reinforce that its powers are present to greatly impact life on earth? What if heaven is giving us lessons on how to march? And what if these lessons aren't about marching out of this life, up to heaven, but out into the world? What if God's burning passion for us isn't to move people toward heaven, but to move us— His people—into the world as we take heaven with us?

The people of Ephesus were taught that because Jesus descended, He also ascended. And often that is where we leave it. That He came down and He went back up.

But that's not where the book of Ephesians leaves it. Ephesians 4:10 says that Jesus ascended "in order to fill the whole universe." He went up so that He could spread His goodness everywhere. His going up wasn't about going away. Instead, He was positioning Himself to spread restoration, redemption, and hope throughout the world.

Sara Groves has become one of our favorite Christian recording artists. Her voice is quietly powerful, winsome, effortless, and authentic. And she has a heart that creates lyrics that stimulate the imagination and call people to action.

I don't know what events led her to write the song "When the Saints," but it is a work of pure genius. To tweak the lyrics of a famous song is no easy task, especially a song such as "When the Saints Go Marching In," which has been performed by Elvis Presley, Louis Armstrong, Judy Garland, Bruce Springsteen, and Dolly Parton. Before Sara was born, the song had already made its way through every genre and had crossed barriers of race, age, and religious affiliations. "Lord, how I want to be in that number, when the saints go marching in."[3]

But Sara Groves took hold of the song and flipped it. With carefully crafted words and image after image of historical bravery, she created a song that redefined what it means to march. She gave the world a song about running *into* injustice, not from it.

She wove together images of the Underground Railroad, the martyrs of Ecuador, and Mother Teresa of Calcutta, before landing a final blow that still brings tears to my eyes:

> I see the young girl huddled on the brothel floor
> I see the man with a passion come and kicking down
>   that door.[4]

If Sara Groves is right, Jesus does not invite us to fly away on wings, but to march with determination. For every girl oppressed in a brothel, there's a door that needs to be kicked down. Ever since the door of the tomb was kicked down and Jesus came back to life, the clock has been ticking on injustice. We, the church, have become His working agents.

Sara doesn't sing about a person with power or influence. She didn't praise someone who was able to get a thousand signatures on a petition or a law passed by Congress. A saint is simply someone with passion. Scripture teaches us that God can do extraordinary things with a passionate heart.

In his book *Rich Christians in an Age of Hunger,* Ronald Sider wrote about Northeast High in Philadelphia. At one time, this high school was famous for its academic standards and athletic accomplishments. It was the second-oldest school in the city, and classes were taught by excellent teachers. Then, black Philadelphians moved to that part of the city. When that happened, many of the white residents fled to other parts of town.

As white families moved away, the name of Northeast High also moved. It was given to a new school built in 1957 in another part of the city. Educators were given the option to transfer to the new school, and two-thirds of them did.

The high school in the old neighborhood was renamed Edison High.

For years, it struggled to find teachers and adequate educational materials. As a result, academics suffered.

But Edison High holds one record, and it has to do with bravery. More students from Edison died in the Army fighting in the Vietnam War than students from any other U.S. high school. Fifty-four young men from Edison lost their lives in Southeast Asia.[5]

Heroes can come from anywhere. Their names may never be known, and their stories may never be told. But they march from safety into risk. They run into injustice, not from it.

I don't know Sara Groves, but I would assume she isn't as interested in how her song makes people feel as much as she's interested in what the song leads people to do. Feelings come and go within minutes. Actions are what change the world.

ENGAGING, NOT ESCAPING, THE WORLD

Have you ever noticed that Jesus in the four Gospels—and His disciples in the book of Acts—healed more cases of blindness and physical disabilities involving mobility than any other illness? Why such an obsession with eyes and legs? I'm not suggesting He ranked illnesses or that He had more compassion for someone who couldn't see than He did for someone who couldn't speak. But I think Scripture wants us to understand how important it is for us to have eyes that see right and legs that move in order to accomplish the work of the Kingdom.

Which is why Paul, in writing to the people living in Ephesus, hit them with "finally" in chapter 6. He had one more message to share. Leading up to this, he devoted three chapters to our identity—who we are in Christ and the identity of the church. Then he listed more than thirty-five commands given to challenge us to live right and to set the world right. Our new identity in Jesus leads us to engagement in His mission.

Which brings us to chapter 6 verse 10, the final message about our standing firm, then marching forward clothed in God's armor: "Finally, be strong in the Lord and in his mighty power." This is not a war in which we flee evil while, at the same time, run into the world to spread the love of Jesus. This war requires armor.

If you look closely at the armor of God, you see that every part of the body gets covered, except the back. There are at least two reasons for this. One, you don't fight alone, which means a comrade has your back and you have his or hers. In that era, shields often would interlock with other shields to form a larger, stronger unified front. You would be foolish to enter battle without your comrades.

But perhaps Paul had a second reason in mind when he wrote this passage. Maybe there is no armor to protect your back *because to walk away from the world is to walk away from the ways of God*. Maybe God wants us all to know that when we refuse to march into the world to engage it with purpose and passion, we are exposed and vulnerable to the powers of darkness. It's a dangerous thing to turn your back when you have the opportunity to right a wrong, to minister to someone with compassion, or to address injustice in the world.

I do not want God to ask me, *Josh, why did you always play it safe?* One thing I've learned from reading the life and teachings of Jesus is that choosing safety and comfort over risk taking and engagement isn't always of God. We see this in the letter to the Ephesians. For the church in Ephesus, it wasn't a matter of "Will we?" engage our city, but "What should we wear?" as we enter the engagement.

The Jesus-followers marched, and so do we. If it is true that ultimately God wants to restore the world to its original painless and deathless state, then perhaps the process already has begun. We can be sure of one thing: we all have significant roles to play.

3

The Groans of Creation

Heaven Is a Reality Defined by God's Will Being Done

Man is the only animal that laughs and
weeps, for he is the only animal that is struck
with the difference between what things are
and what things ought to be.

— William Hazlitt

I know much less about why God allows
people to suffer than I know that He Himself
is a suffering God.

— Jonathan Martin

The first time I (Jonathan) got mad at God I was in my midtwenties. It was a few weeks after the historic tsunami that killed hundreds of thousands of people in Southeast Asia. When my wife and I traveled with a team of people to do relief work, we had no idea what hell we were running toward.

We met people there who had lost everything. One guy had been riding a train that was pushed onto its side and soon was flooded with water. He was the only person who survived. Leslie and I met a boy named Suresh who lost every family member except his little sister. At thirteen, he was the man of the house now.

Probably the most tragic moment of all, the moment when it all seemed to crash in on me, came when I was alone on a beach. We had been there for just a few days, and we were doing cleanup in the most hard-hit place in the world. As I picked up items off a beach, I found some shoes buried underneath a heap of trash. They had belonged to a little girl.

I couldn't avoid picturing the scene. Little girls were playing near the beach on a Sunday morning. And before anyone could issue an alarm or run to help them, the girls were gasping for breath and buried beneath the raging sea.

God could have stopped the tectonic plates from shifting, preventing the upheaval that triggered the incredible destructive force. He could have made the giant wave stop before it covered shorelines and came far inland to wipe out towns. He could have, but He didn't.

One moment I was working to clean up a beach, the next I was facing an existential crisis. A tragedy that had been all over the news, hundreds of thousands dead in a far-off land, was no longer an abstract problem. It had suddenly become the tragic reality I was holding in my hands.

Did you ever wonder why the Bible ends with God coming down, and at that point it mentions that in the new heaven and new earth there will be *no more sea*? I used to question that omission, but not anymore.

For the ancient Jewish mind, the sea was the symbol of chaos. The ancient world knew what we don't. But people today who make their life and death by the sea know it as well: the sea is not always a good vacationing spot. It gives and it takes away.

People in the ancient world thought of the sea as the Abyss. It was evil. All of us can understand evil.

We have attended too many funerals and seen too many disasters, both up close and a world away, to pretend that the world is okay. The struggle is to understand why the God we believe is good would allow any of this.

Right after the Fall, God made sure to tell Adam and Eve that creation had fundamentally changed because they had disobeyed His command. They knew then, and we know now, that we should expect evil on earth.

To Adam he said, "Because you listened to your wife and ate fruit from the tree about which I commanded you, 'You must not eat from it,'

"Cursed is the ground because of you;
  through painful toil you will eat food from it
  all the days of your life.
It will produce thorns and thistles for you,
  and you will eat the plants of the field.
By the sweat of your brow
  you will eat your food
until you return to the ground,
  since from it you were taken;
for dust you are
  and to dust you will return." (Genesis 3:17–19)

There are thorns and thistles, hurricanes and tsunamis, and principalities and powers. The world is deeply broken. This could go a long way toward explaining why bad things keep happening. For instance, why the New England Patriots have won so many Super Bowls!

A HAUNTED WORLD

The God of the Old Testament stood apart from the gods of the polytheistic cultures of the ancient Near East. The Hebrew Scriptures taught that God was not only more powerful than other powers, but that He was the God who created every other power. Even at that, however, the Jews realized that all powers on earth were not yet—at least at the operational level—submitted to God.

When talk turns to principalities and powers—unseen spiritual forces that oppose God and war against the people of God—I realize it sounds primitive. We live in the modern world after all, where we have penicillin, Hondas, and PlayStation 4. We live in a time when science and technology have explained away all the things that can't be seen or touched. Given the world we live in—the advanced state of knowledge that characterizes our culture—it can be hard to read the biblical story without missing a large chunk of what is being said.

Think about this: is it possible that we have simply given new names to the powers and principalities? Philip Yancey wrote these words:

> [How do we] explain the rationale behind the overnight collapse of
> economies in Asia and Latin America, or a sniper who starts picking
> off suburbanites at shopping malls and gas stations? What keeps a
> wealthy nation like the United States from finding shelter for its
> homeless population? What keeps the world from feeding the
> thousands who die malnourished each day? The experts have no
> answer [other than] "forces beyond our control." The New Testa-
> ment writers agree and do not hesitate to identify those factors.[1]

We have so mastered our world that we can fool ourselves into thinking we have everything figured out. We believe that if we can define it, categorize it, and make it fit into a bigger scheme or accepted theory, then we can control it.

But the biblical idea of creation does not conform to the modern worldview. We can't just keep improving conditions in the world until there is no more death or suffering. Having the right political positions, achieving another scientific breakthrough, or improving education for all—none of these will fix everything. That is because the problem is buried deep within all of us and in every atom of creation. The solutions we are accustomed to, and which we look to as the hope of the world, are powerless in the face of the universal, inherent problem.

Most of the conversations we have about God are based on what theologians call Deism, the idea that God and heaven are somewhere else. Deism teaches that God created the universe, set it in motion, then stepped outside it.

Even Christians believe this at a fundamental level. Whenever we suspect that God has reached in and tinkered with events on earth, we refer to it as a miracle. The unspoken assumption is that, whenever the affairs of the world are moving along as usual, God is somewhere else, absent from creation.

But that's not the way the Bible talks about God and the world.

In Genesis, when we read the creation account, the Garden of Eden is described as a kind of royal garden. Earth is cast as heaven's backyard. And while things have changed dramatically since creation, heaven and earth still sometimes overlap and interconnect.

In the Christian worldview, heaven is the realm in which everything is as God wills; it is not just a far-off location out past Jupiter. Heaven is less a location and more a reality defined by God's will being done. Yet here on earth, a lot of people are working against heaven by trying to make sure that what *they will* is what gets done.

Still, heaven breaks through on earth. God's mission is to partner with people in the task of bringing the two realities—earth and heaven—back together.

God asked Adam and Eve to tend to creation, but they disobeyed. As the history of the world began to unfold, God called Abraham's family (later forming the nation of Israel) to do what Adam and Eve couldn't.

God had called the first people He created to live out His intentions on earth. They failed at the task. Much later, God still wanted to show the world what His original intention was. He still wanted to reveal what life under the reign of the good and only God looked like. That was His calling given to Abraham and to Abraham's descendants, but repeatedly they disobeyed.

Throughout human history it is evident that the problem of evil isn't just "out there." It is in us too.

TEMPTATION ON EARTH

What are we to do with the opening story in the Gospel of Matthew? Matthew wrote that before Jesus did any public ministry, He went into the wilderness for forty days. Who would have seen that coming? God's Son, having prepared for three years of His life, didn't jump immediately into ministry. Instead He wandered into the desert (see Matthew 4:1–11).

So much of Jesus's ministry is a bit like street theater. He cursed a fig tree, then the next time His disciples saw it, it had shriveled up. Jesus healed people on the Sabbath, in public, in front of everyone, in direct violation of well-known Jewish tradition.

Perhaps His forty days in the desert aren't all that surprising after all. He came out of the experience and reached the Jordan River, where He was baptized . . . just like Israel did in Joshua 3. Jesus's earthly life mirrored the story of Israel. He showed humanity that what Adam and Eve—and later Israel—failed to do in response to God, He was finally fulfilling.

Jesus's ministry was powered by the forty days He spent in the desert being tempted by Satan. He endured the temptations, overcame them, and bound up the strong man. His ministry shows us what work on earth looks like when actions, motivations, and priorities are not controlled by evil. Everywhere Jesus went, He overcame evil and set the world right.

Jesus is the faithful Human, and He showed us how to do what we were created to do. We are to steward God's world and to exercise loving dominion over creation.

If that seems too lofty and unreachable, consider that Jesus had ordinary people share in what He was doing. For instance, He sent seventy followers out to do ministry, to preach, and to heal. When they returned from this mission, they told Jesus that even demons submitted to them in His name (see Luke 10:17). Jesus responded with something I find amazing:

> I saw Satan fall like lightning from heaven. I have given you
> authority to trample on snakes and scorpions and to overcome all
> the power of the enemy; nothing will harm you. However, do not
> rejoice that the spirits submit to you, but rejoice that your names
> are written in heaven. (Luke 10:18–20)

The disciples had been walking over hot sand, knocking on doors, asking to see the sick, announcing the coming of Jesus. All their actions took place in the visible world, which they could touch, smell, and see. But Jesus saw a lot more happening. He saw that the actions in the visible world were having a startling impact on the invisible world. What we do has both personal and cosmological implications.

THE SAINTS ARE CHEERING

Let's take this further. In Revelation 5, we read about what happens in heaven when we pray. At first it seems a bit . . . underwhelming. Revelation tells us that the prayers of the saints become bowls of incense (see 5:8, NIV 1984).

I have always imagined that the prayer of God's people would shake the earth, close the mouths of lions, or cure cancer. But in Revelation John tells us it smells nice. Mark Buchanan, in his book *Your God Is Too Safe,* calls our attention to what happens to these prayers just a few chapters later in Revelation:

> Another angel, who had a golden censer, came and stood at the altar. He was given much incense to offer, with the prayers of all the saints, on the golden altar before the throne. The smoke of the incense, together with the prayers of the saints, went up before God from the angel's hand. Then the angel took the censer, filled it with fire from the altar, and hurled it on the earth; and there came peals of thunder, rumblings, flashes of lightning, and an earthquake.[2]

Thunder, earthquakes, and lightning (oh my). The prayers of the saints turn into bombs.

Author and churchman William Willimon has told about a time when a friend of his traveled with a group of people to Russia during the Cold War. They were touring churches in Russia to see how Christians were faring in a rigid atheistic society. Willimon's friend came back and reported, "The church [in Russia] was mostly 'irrelevant because the only people there are little old ladies.'"[3]

But Willimon says in hindsight, his friend should have known better. Visit Russia today and you will walk past the crumbling statues of Stalin and Lenin. But the church rolls on, in part because of those sweet old ladies.

We should know, from reading the Scripture, that little old ladies who pray are secret revolutionaries. Because heaven is connected to earth, believers who pray are a bomb-making factory.

There is an overlap and interconnection between heaven and earth, and what we do on earth matters in heaven. Likewise, what happens there matters here. When New Testament writers corresponded with churches that were facing persecution, with the believers looking evil dead in the face, the biblical writers tried to give them a glimpse of what was going on in the heavens at that moment.

The writer to the Hebrews let persecuted Christians know about the great cloud of witnesses that was (and is still) cheering them on. John, writing Revelation, was addressing persecuted Christians in the first century. He encouraged them by giving them a glimpse into the heavenlies.

The New Testament writers did not introduce stories of heaven as a way to distract those who were suffering from the evil on earth. Rather, the New Testament writers wanted believers in the first century, and you and I as well, to know that God, the angels, and the saints in heaven are paying attention to us!

Speaking of heaven, some of you may remember a few years ago when the Dallas Mavericks were playing the Miami Heat for the NBA championship. Classic good versus evil, right?

Toward the end of the fourth quarter, the ABC sports commentators started showing video feed of the American Airlines Center, but not the one in Miami (where the game was being played). Instead, they were showing the one in Dallas. It was filled with thousands of people who were watching the game on a big screen. Of course, the Mavericks couldn't see their fans who had gathered back home.

Meanwhile, in Miami, Dallas was down by fifteen with just a few minutes to go. They were playing in a hostile environment: everyone in the stands was cheering against them. But just a commercial flight away thousands of people were gathered to watch the game projected on a screen. And they were cheering their heads off for their beloved Mavericks. This is similar to what the Scripture writers wanted us to see.

You may be going through a dark season, you may feel isolated and alone, but you are not unnoticed and you are never alone. The heavens are cheering you on. In another realm an unseen group of people is rooting for you to accomplish God's plans of bringing the heavenlies to earth. Moses and Abraham, grandmothers and departed friends, all the saints who went before you. The great cloud of witnesses cheers you on from heaven. And it isn't as far away as you might think.

Joining the Groan of Creation

At the time I (Jonathan) was writing this book with Josh, Leslie and I found out we were pregnant again. We had been, you know, "practicing" for a while. We were pretty stoked about adding a new member to the Storment family.

We started to share our news right after the first trimester was coming to an end.

And then, well into our fourth month, I went with Leslie to the doctor to find out the gender and to hear the heartbeat.

But they couldn't find it. And we couldn't find our breath. It felt like the rug got yanked from under us. Our little girl was never going to be born. And we groaned with the rest of creation.

In her brilliant book *Joy Unspeakable*, Barbara Holmes talks about the language of the "moan." It was a language birthed from slavery, an inhumane practice dating to ancient times. The Hebrews were slaves in Egypt. And in our own nation's history, there is the blot of slavery.

Africans were placed on slave ships, forced to leave their communities, and brought to live in a new land not as people, but as property. The journey from Africa to America often is referred to as the journey across bitter waters—not because of the ocean, but because of the trauma. As these kidnapped souls were chained to one another, lying on their sides in the bowels of a ship, a new language was birthed. Many of the Africans didn't speak the same language. They came from different tribes and cultures, but on the ships they began to speak a common language—*the moan.*

Holmes describes it like this: "The moan becomes the vehicle for articulating that which can never be voiced. . . . [M]oans are the utterances of choice when circumstances snatch words and prayers from bereft lips. . . . On the slave ships the moan became the language of stolen strangers, the articulation of unspeakable fears, the precursor to joy yet unknown."[4]

It's a language still heard in African American settings. You hear it in worship services, in response to a preacher's words, or during prayer. Maybe you've witnessed this in the powerful campfire scene in the movie *Glory,* as the 54th Massachusetts Volunteer Infantry prepared for an engagement that would take the life of every other Union soldier headed into battle. It's the moan, groan, and lament you hear in the hip-hop songs of Tupac, Jay-Z, and Lecrae.

Meaning that is uttered because it cannot be spoken echoes from the slave ships. It can be traced all the way back to the Israelites, whose groaning was heard by the Lord while they were slaves in Egypt. Today it is the language spoken by young girls in brothels, young slaves fishing on lakes in Ghana, and from the single mom who is doing her best to raise four children on her own.

It is the language that comes from a young couple who just found out their baby's heart stopped beating while in her mother's womb.

Jesus was familiar with the moan.

JESUS GROANED FOR THIS WORLD TO BE RESTORED

A deaf man approached Jesus. He wanted to be healed, but he couldn't communicate his desires. Jesus took the man aside, then spat on His hands. Jesus touched the man's tongue and placed His fingers in the man's ears. It's the only time we know of that Jesus gave somebody a wet willy. As interesting as this is, Jesus did not use the same method to heal anyone else.

Tim Keller has written that Jesus was entering the man's cognitive realm. He made Himself as accessible as possible. He communicated with the man nonverbally, the only way the deaf man could understand. Furthermore, He took the man away from the crowd. The guy had probably been mocked his entire life, and Jesus refused to let that happen again.[5]

Before He restored the man's hearing, Jesus sighed. The Greek word that describes this is a rare word that means Jesus Himself hurt for the man. There was deep compassion in Jesus that responded to the man's suffering.

An even better translation of this would be that Jesus *groaned*. I love that idea. The Son of God, the One who came to redeem the earth, was groaning with the deaf man. Today, Jesus is groaning with us.

All of creation, from Jupiter to the Grand Canyon to white blood cells, anticipates this world's being set right. All of creation *groans* for that to happen. Jesus, even now, joins with creation in the groaning.

In the heavens, the cloud of witnesses cheers us on. Jesus Himself joins with them. Jesus is watching us take the hits, and He cheers us on as we move God's good creation project forward.

SATAN FALLS LIKE LIGHTNING

Perhaps you have traveled to parts of the world where children are dying because they lack simple necessities, such as food or water. And maybe you thought: *Where is God?*

I have a young friend named Elizabeth who heard stories about children who had no access to clean water. So she gave up her birthday presents. When she turned eight, instead of asking for presents, she requested that the people who were coming to celebrate her life give money to charity so that other people could have life.

The party guests did just that. They raised money to dig a well in Africa.

A few years ago the people of Myanmar (Burma) suffered the devastation of a horrible cyclone. If you are like me, when you heard about it or saw pictures of the devastation, you wondered where God was when the winds were laying waste to that region. And while all that was going on, my friend Jon Joncs was there. He goes to Myanmar to work with the people, trying to get them food. He told me that he can't see an American dollar anymore without thinking about how much rice it will buy.

My wife used to work alongside an old college friend—we call him Bad Brad—at a Christian children's home in inner-city Fort Worth. If you have ever served in that ministry, you know the joy and the exhaustion this kind of work brings.

One week in particular stands out to both of them: it was the week when they met Ricky. When Ricky first came to the home, they learned he had been abused by a number of people before he had turned four. Every other word he uttered was a profanity. But what was most jarring is that Ricky often would ask: "Would you like to have sex with me?"

He had been taught that his only value was found in his ability to gratify the evil desires of people who held authority over him. Before he could ride a roller coaster, swim, or read, Ricky had been initiated into the darkest evil of the world.

My wife and Bad Brad discovered that this sweet little boy couldn't go to sleep at night because he was consumed by fear. The only way to get him to sleep without drugs was by reading him stories. He was fond of *The Big Brown Bear*. It's a classic.

When I hear about this small boy, harmed terribly by people bent on doing evil, I wonder, *Where is God?* But then God gave me new eyes to see what was going on.

I'll tell you where God is. He is reading stories to Ricky so a traumatized boy can fall asleep at night. God is moving through a Burmese refugee camp, distributing rice to as many people as possible. God is in Elizabeth, at the age of eight, giving up her birthday gifts to help other kids.

That's where God is. And I see Satan falling like lightning.

The drug dealer and the AIDS baby. The single mom and the spotted owl. The cancer patient and the convict. The woman on welfare and the CEO. The couple who can't have kids, and the parents who just lost one.

We all are groaning, waiting on God's people to partner with God in His new-creation project. The broken creation that God intended to operate according to His will—as things do in heaven—will be restored on earth. We groan as we wait for the new creation to appear.

That is how heaven invades earth. That is when the world will be set right, and death will pay back what it owes. There will be no more empty shoes of little girls buried under trash on a beach. Because in the restored world, there will be no more sea.

4

Heaven Is Not the End of the World

Why Does Talk About Heaven Make It Seem Less Real Than Earth?

> Ooh, baby, do you know what that's
> worth? . . . We'll make heaven a place
> on earth.
>
> — Belinda Carlisle

In the 1960s, testifying before the US Supreme Court, atheist Madalyn Murray O'Hair had to define what atheism is. Mrs. O'Hair said, "An atheist believes that a hospital should be built instead of a church. An atheist believes that deed must be done instead of prayer said. An atheist strives for involvement in life and not escape into death. He wants disease conquered, poverty vanished, war eliminated."[1]

People of God's Kingdom who want to bring heaven to earth read Mrs. O'Hair's remarks and think, *We kind of believe that too.* She was no friend of the church, but it's hard to read her Supreme Court testimony and not agree with it.

She pointed out, without saying it, that Christians have become dis-connected from life on earth. And I wonder if Mrs. O'Hair realized it wasn't always this way.

Most of the hospitals in the West were started by churches. Prison reform, women's suffrage, child labor laws, the abolition of slavery—all of these were heavily influenced and led by Jesus-followers. Throughout history, God's people have been active in confronting injustice and work-ing to make life on earth different, better, more just. This is essential, and it points to the importance of how we interpret the Bible. If we are con-vinced that God is planning to destroy the world and most of the people He created, we might be reluctant to invest our lives in helping to bring His Kingdom to earth. If in the near future the earth will be obliterated in divine judgment, we might decide to not bother with combating human trafficking, to not fight for the rights of women, or to not try to protect children from exploitation.

If this world doesn't matter, then why should we really care? Which was exactly Mrs. O'Hair's point.

And she was kind of right.

A couple of years ago, I (Jonathan) began noticing billboards throughout Texas that screamed, "THE WORLD IS ENDING ON MAY 21st. ARE YOU READY?"[2]

Really? We're sure about the date?

It reminds me of a houseguest we hosted when I was a teenager grow-ing up in Arkansas. Simran Gujral was a Sikh from India, and he lived with us for about a year.

Sikhs, as you might know, never cut their hair and are known for wearing turbans. Simran was close to my age: we fought and loved each other like brothers. In fact, I still see him every couple of years. He will always be family.

Not that I was always so generous when I was a teenager. There weren't a lot of Sikhs roaming the rural town in Arkansas where I grew up. I was a teenager who desperately wanted to appear normal, but my Sikh brother made me stand out. Still, having Simran around had its advantages. Namely he helped out with my love life.

Back then, my friends and I would roam Wal-Mart on Friday nights looking for romantic opportunities. Classy, right? When we would see a girl we wanted to talk to, we'd send Simran over speaking Punjabi. After a few moments we'd walk over and "translate" what Simran was saying. It sounds like a Nicholas Sparks novel, I know.[3]

Those were bonding experiences, and one day Simran and I were discussing when the world was going to end. He told me stories about Nostradamus and the Mayans, and he mentioned ancient predictions that would be fulfilled in only a few short years.

I believed him. He was, after all, wearing a turban.

But I don't believe it any longer. If the Mayans were able to predict the future, there would still be Mayans. They could have seen the Spanish conquistadores long before they were within sight and prepared their defenses accordingly.

GETTING BEYOND CLOUDS AND HARPS

So what is heaven? Anthropologists say every known culture has some belief in the afterlife. Each culture may have a different name for it, and the descriptions vary, but there is a sense in which God has planted eternity in the human heart.

Throughout Christian history, Jesus-followers have talked about what will happen in the Age to Come. During the first few generations of the Jesus movement, the resurrection was the central focus. The people held on to this hope as they looked death squarely in the face. They were confident that the hope of resurrection meant God was not finished with them, despite what the swords of Rome tried to force them to believe.

But over the centuries, the people of God have thought and talked about the Age to Come in a variety of ways. This is especially true for views advanced during the past couple of hundred years in America. Christians have started to talk about heaven in ways that make it sound like a sterile doctor's office in the sky. Instead of an active, engaging life in God's presence, we picture a solemn, antiseptic atmosphere. Clouds and harps and gold everywhere—nothing like a robust experience of life eternal. We have dismissed spontaneity, adventure, and real life in the Age to Come. Heaven ends up coming across a lot like *The Lawrence Welk Show*.[4]

L.A. Times journalist Joel Stein is known among Christians as being controversial. A couple of years ago, he campaigned for Starbucks to put a quote of his on their paper cups. It said:

> Heaven is totally overrated. It seems boring. Clouds, listening to
> people play the harp. It should be somewhere you can't wait to go,
> like a luxury hotel. Maybe blue skies and soft music were enough
> to keep people in line in the 17th century, but heaven has to step
> it up a bit. They're basically getting by because they only have to
> be better than hell.[5]

Stein is right. Most of the ways we talk about heaven make it appear to be a place *less real* than the place we live in now. Even in popular movies that portray the afterlife, heaven doesn't look very appealing. Consider the movie *Bruce Almighty,* in which Morgan Freeman is stuck in some weird building that looks like a Progressive commercial.

A few years ago, 81 percent of Americans who responded to a survey said they thought heaven was going to be nonmaterial, and that we would be ethereal, or ghost-like.[6] But Scripture never uses such terms when describing heaven.

When the writers of Scripture talked about Jesus's return, they often used metaphors. Sometimes they focused on heaven; a lot of times they focused on earth. Other times they talked about Jesus's return as a banquet, a wedding, or a city.

It's as if there is not just one way of talking about it—no one metaphor—that is big enough to grasp what God is going to do. It's too big to reduce to just one description. And to be sure, we all see through a glass darkly: nobody can be certain about the details.

But hope is important as it relates to the Age to Come. What you hope for is what you will live toward.

WHAT DOES IT MEAN TO BE A CHRISTIAN?

In 1994, Rwanda was the scene of the worst genocide since the Holocaust. The Tutsis, a minority tribe in Rwanda, were massacred at the hands of Hutus. It is estimated that as much as three-quarters of the Tutsi population perished.[7] The worst part of this is that at the time, Rwanda was the most Christianized nation on the planet.

Ninety percent of the country's population in 1994 claimed to follow Jesus. Still, there are stories of entire church congregations rising up to kill people from another tribe who also were members of Christian churches. How could this be?[8]

You can't escape the disturbing contradiction: If Christians were executing innocent fellow Christians, then what does it mean to be a Christian? Rwandan believers understood the gospel to point toward a future

reality, heaven, after they died. But their faith clearly didn't have implications for the way they lived on earth.

Christians have asked this question for far too long: If you were to die
tonight, where would you go? We need to start asking, if you wake up
tomorrow morning, what will you live for? For too long we have mea-
sured our love for another person based on whether we would die for her.
Maybe the better is, Do you love someone so much you will live for him?

At the time of the Rwandan genocide, the African nation was celebrated by American missionaries as representing a model of success.
Clearly, the problem that existed was being overlooked. The people said
they believed the message of Jesus, but they had been taught a different
kind of message about Jesus. They knew about going to heaven, but not
much about whether people should or should not kill their neighbor.[9]

Dallas Willard made this point well:

> The current situation in which faith professed has little impact on
> the whole of life is not unique to our times, nor is it a recent
> development. But it is currently at an acute stage. History has
> brought us to the point where the Christian message is thought to
> be *essentially* concerned *only* with how to deal with sin: with
> wrongdoing or wrong-being and its effects. Life, our actual
> existence, is not included in what is now presented as the heart of
> the Christian message. . . . That is where we find ourselves today.[10]

We seem to think Jesus knows a lot about getting us to heaven, but
not much about how we should live while we reside on earth. We have
split the world into the sacred and the profane, the physical and spiritual,
heaven and earth. But that is a distinction the Scriptures never make. In
fact, such dualism in ancient times was known as a major heresy.

HAVE WE TURNED INTO GNOSTICS?

One of the first Christian heresies that we know about is an idea called Gnosticism. It held that a human is a divine soul trapped in a material world. In order to free oneself from the material world, you had to have special knowledge that was available only to the elite. If you were one of the enlightened ones, after you died you would escape this world and turn into a spiritual being freed from the flesh.

In *The Da Vinci Code,* novelist Dan Brown indicated that the church squashed the Gnostic heresy in order to hold back a revolution. The truth is just the opposite. The church fought this idea because widespread acceptance of Gnosticism would have *stopped* the revolution.

For the Gnostics, the flesh was the product of a bad creation. They viewed God's creation as such a bad thing that they started to tell people that Jesus didn't come in the flesh—that He was, in fact, just a spirit. Because the material world was thought to be bad, God obviously wouldn't have come to earth in bodily form. This world, our bodies, and how we live our lives all are irrelevant, because the real mission and purposes of God are somewhere else—in the future after we die. Thus is the heresy of Gnosticism.

Christian hope is that God entered this very world to redeem it, so actual matter . . . well, matters!

Gnosticism was, in fact, a form of escaping reality by dismissing it. A Gnostic idea of heaven is that one day we will become spiritual beings and start living outside this world as spirits in another realm. Does that sound familiar?

Remember, this was the first major heresy.

Thankfully we have the Christian story, which begins with a God who says repeatedly that creation is good. He likes what He made. There's more. The prophets never talked about heaven as some kind of blurry, esoteric realm located far from earth. They spoke of a new heaven and a new earth, referring to a time in the future when this earth would be restored and renewed. At that time, all things and people would be reconciled to one another and to God.[11]

Jesus spoke of the future in a similar way. In Matthew 19:28, He talked about the Age to Come. Notice the words He reached for: "Truly I tell you, at the renewal of all things, when the Son of Man sits on his glorious throne . . ."

At the renewal of all things. The Greek here uses two words, *Pali-Genesis*. *Genesis* meaning "beginning," and *Pali* meaning "again." Genesis again.

New Lessons from Creation

God has never given up on His original creation, but His people seem to from time to time. We have overlooked the vocabulary that the Bible gave us. Think about the words the Bible uses to describe God's plans for us: *redeem, resurrect, restore, renew, recover, regenerate.*[12]

Each of these words means "to return to a previous state."

God is the ultimate Salvage Artist. He loves to restore, redeem, and renew things that everyone else has written off as irreversibly broken or dead. God loves resurrection.

But certain teachings downplay this biblical emphasis in favor of the coming destruction of the world. For nearly two hundred years, Christians in the West have been influenced by end-times teachings that emphasize the Rapture. This is not a word that appears in the Bible, but the idea behind it has great appeal.

The idea has been in circulation for only a tiny portion of the church's history. Prior to that, the accepted theology of the church embraced the mystery of the Age to Come, but also its continuity with the created world. For the past century and a half, however, much of the imagination of Western Christianity has been captured by theories regarding the thousand-year reign mentioned in Revelation 20.[13]

It's legitimate to argue whether the book of Revelation was meant to be taken literally. We believe the great tragedy of overemphasizing a minor passage regarding the Rapture is that it has prevented Christians from engaging the very world that God says is good. When Christians believe that God will judge the world but that they will be carried away in advance of the worst judgments, it shifts their focus away from God's restoring work on earth.

We believe that the real R-word of the New Testament is not *rapture*, which is never mentioned, but *resurrection*, which is mentioned more than forty times. For almost two thousand years, the church's leading thinkers and teachers did not believe in the Rapture. It is an idea that was foreign to the teachings of Augustine, Calvin, Luther, and Wesley. Teachings that center on the Rapture appeared recently, originating with an Anglo-Irish evangelist named John Darby. He taught that Jesus would return twice but that His first second coming would be in secret, when He would come to take away all Christians to heaven.

Darby made several trips to the United States in the 1800s, and his teachings began to catch on in a big way. I mean *really catch on*. Today, a group of atheists offer pet-sitting services for a mere $115. They promise to come rescue your pet post-Rapture. Their business is expanding.

Another business—this one operated by Christians—offers a system whereby your heathen friends and family members can be notified that you have been raptured. (Thus, if they are reading the message, they have been left behind.) For an annual fee of $14.95, your prewritten message will automatically be sent out if three of the five Christians who maintain the database don't log in for a six-day period.

Again, this is for real.

I know the Rapture teaching started out with good intentions, but it's important to remember that what we direct our hope toward greatly affects how we practice our faith. Further, a belief that emphasizes the stealthy escape of believers from earth before a global, end-times conflagration destroys what God created is not consistent with classic Christian doctrine.

What you hope for shapes what you live for.

Why should Christians care for the earth's environment if God is just going to beam all of us up to heaven to get us out of the way before He destroys the universe? Why should we fight for justice and compassion on earth if God's bigger plan is to wait until eternity before anyone can get his or her reward?

The escapist idea contradicts not just Jesus's teachings, but also His earthly (and earthy) life and practices. He was fully God and fully human, and His human side was decidedly not removed from our ordinary, troubled world. He enjoyed food and drink with friends and strangers alike. He walked miles in a hot, arid land. He sweated, got dirty, got tired and hungry. He needed friends, went out of His way to reach people, responded to very real human needs.

Jesus repeatedly told His closest followers that He would return to His Father. Meanwhile, He emphasized their role and involvement in God's Kingdom on earth. He did not minimize the needs of people by pointing to a future payoff in heaven. Working for justice, being guided by compassion, sacrificing yourself for the good of others in this life—all of these were modeled by Jesus and emphasized in His teachings.

American Christianity is anemic when it comes to helping Christians become the kind of people who look and act like Jesus. After all, why should we live that differently on earth if the gospel is mostly about living somewhere else?

Is heaven a place that is far removed from earth, an ethereal, otherworldly realm that bears little resemblance to the world we live in? Let's revisit Scripture to find out. Paul talked a lot about the resurrection of Jesus. Most of the time he framed it in the Exodus story. In Romans 8:26, for example, Paul wrote that all of creation is groaning, longing for its redemption from slavery. In 1 Corinthians 15, the longest section in the Bible about the resurrection, he wrote that the resurrection of Jesus is the "firstfruits" of a larger thing God is going to do (verse 20). *Firstfruits* is a reference to a holiday that the Jews celebrated, one that centered around the Exodus story.

This is important, because after the Israelites were freed from slavery, they went up to meet with God on a mountain.

On the morning of the third day there was thunder and lightning, with a thick cloud over the mountain, and a very loud trumpet blast. Everyone in the camp trembled. Then Moses led the people out of the camp to meet with God, and they stood at the foot of the mountain. Mount Sinai was covered with smoke, because the LORD descended on it in fire. The smoke billowed up from it like smoke from a furnace, and the whole mountain trembled violently. As the sound of the trumpet grew louder and louder, Moses spoke and the voice of God answered him.

The LORD descended to the top of Mount Sinai and called Moses to the top of the mountain. So Moses went up. (Exodus 19:16–20)

God met with the Israelites at a mountain, in a cloud, and there was a trumpet. If we keep that in mind, 1 Thessalonians 4 has a different sound.

Brothers and sisters, we do not want you to be uninformed about those who sleep in death, so that you do not grieve like the rest of mankind, who have no hope. For we believe that Jesus died and rose again, and so we believe that God will bring with Jesus those who have fallen asleep in him. According to the Lord's word, we tell you that we who are still alive, who are left until the coming of the Lord, will certainly not precede those who have fallen asleep. For the Lord himself will come down from heaven, with a loud command, with the voice of the archangel and with the trumpet call of God, and the dead in Christ will rise first. After that, we who are still alive and are left will be caught up together with them in the clouds to meet the Lord in the air. And so we will be with the Lord forever. Therefore encourage one another with these words. (1 Thessalonians 4:13–18)

When you read that passage with the Exodus story in mind, you will be less likely to hear something that Paul isn't saying. We too often act as if Paul said, "Just hold on until God beams us out of here." But he didn't write that.

Many of us grew up singing: "Somewhere in outer space, God has prepared a place." The name of that children's song is "Blast Off."

When did Spock start writing our worship songs?

In reality, all the talk about God's people being removed from earth to be shot off to heaven is like saying the point of the Exodus story was for the Israelites to stay at the mountain with God. Of course, when we read Exodus, we never expect the Hebrews to remain at the mountain. God had called them out of slavery to live as His people on earth. They would be a people set apart for God, and how they lived would mark them as clearly different from the nations that surrounded them. (At least that was God's intent.) The Jews would serve as witnesses.

Remember, Moses came back from the mountaintop.

Too many Christians have missed this most important lesson. Instead of following the earthly Jesus, connected thoroughly to life on earth, we have invented a theology of escapism. It's Gnostic in its eagerness to separate spiritual life from everyday life. We have developed a disembodied gospel, a gospel with a soul separated from the body. The effect for most Christians in our culture has been to war against the culture rather than to live as salt and light, engaged with people to redeem life on earth. Is it any wonder Christians are thought of so unfavorably?

WHEN HEAVEN WILL CRASH INTO EARTH

In the book of Revelation, John's description of the end times includes heaven coming down. The heavenly city *does not stay in heaven* but rather comes down to earth.[14]

Heaven isn't the end of the world. It's the *beginning* of the world, just as the early church and the leading theologians of the church have always said. In light of this, I can't end this chapter without commenting on the end-of-the-world billboards I used to drive past. The billboard would lead you to a website. If you went there, you would hear people talking about how Noah knew the world was going to end—and "You can too!" To calculate the exact date, just do the appropriate math that is hidden throughout the Bible, use the correct logarithm, and add a touch of crazy. You'll come up with the same date that was arrived at by the sponsor of the billboard message.

The guy in question made this prediction in the past, arriving at different dates back then and returning to his calculations only after the dates came and went and we all were still here. At least he's persistent.[15]

There is a big problem with all this. One of the little-talked-about moments in Jesus's teaching is when He addressed the question of when

He would make His return. He spoke of God's judgment and the Age to Come. In fact, Jesus explained why anyone who sets a date for the Second Coming is lying. "But about that day or hour no one knows, not even the angels in heaven, nor the Son, but only the Father" (Matthew 24:36).

If someone chooses May 21 as the certain time of Jesus's return and Jesus doesn't show up that day, we all know what will happen on May 22. There will still be unrest in the Middle East, homelessness in Abilene, Texas, and people everywhere who are alone, displaced, and suffering.

The church will still be called to do something about all these things. If Jesus fails to return on May 21, your life and mine can be the place where eternity meets the greatest needs on earth.

God has not told us when the Age to Come will come. He knows that if we knew the date we would live for that day and neglect all else. But the call of God is to live for this place and this time. To make there and then come here and now.

Heaven and earth were always meant to be together, and one day they will join fully and finally. Justice will roll like a river, righteousness like a never-ending stream.

Lions will lie down with lambs, and the mountains will clap with joy. This is God's good world, and He hasn't given up on it.

Make yourself at home.

5

The Flames of Heaven

The Gospel Is More About
This World Than the Next

No good thing is destroyed.

— C. S. Lewis

The fires of Heaven may well be hotter for
some than the fires of Hell.

— Dallas Willard

A friend of mine had an affair a few years ago. He had made a series of sinful choices that almost tore his marriage apart. But when he came to his senses, his wife and children forgave him.

I (Jonathan) called him to ask how things were going. I'll never forget what he said: "My wife is committed to the long process of forgiving and putting this behind us. I've been the recipient of unconditional grace. It feels awful."

Grace feels awful?

My friend went on to explain that forgiveness at first feels like condemnation. Grace initially is an indictment, because forgiveness carries with it the luggage of guilt. Only the sick need a doctor. And the work of the doctor is both effective and disturbing.

A CHANGING GRACE

In many places, the local church has made becoming a Christian fairly easy and living as a disciple optional. Jesus didn't envision it ever being this way. Dallas Willard wrote about this trend: "It is now understood to be a part of the 'good news' that one does not have to be a life student of Jesus in order to be a Christian."[1]

Throughout Christian history, the idea of eternal punishment has been used to control people's behavior. But during the Protestant Reformation, when Christians began to reemphasize God's grace, Protestant leaders noticed a lot of people stopped coming to church.

This runs deeper than just church attendance. In his book, *Emotionally Healthy Spirituality,* pastor Peter Scazzero points out there is not a marked difference between Christians in much of life. Christians divorce as much as their secular neighbors, church members are just as likely to beat their spouse as their secular counterparts, the giving patterns of Christians indicate that they are almost as materialistic as non-Christians, and white Evangelicals are the most likely group to object to a person of color moving in to their neighborhood.[2]

Faith seems to have a limited effect on the way most people live when the fear of hell has been removed from the equation.

How did we get to the place where following the most revolutionary Man who ever lived doesn't revolutionize the people who claim to follow Him?

The gospel is more about this world than the next. It is the story of God's work in restoring a broken world and broken people. It is a return to life. And this is good news—no, it's the *best* news—for individual souls, for neighborhoods, for cities, and for the world. As the Kingdom spreads, anything that has set itself up against the will of God is forced to flee.

Don't get us wrong, the gospel is about heaven. But heaven is not the distant, otherworldly place we often imagine it to be. Heaven will come down to earth. We will live on earth in a renewed, restored world.

DOES THIS REALLY SOUND LIKE GOOD NEWS?

For some of us, the idea of heaven coming to earth and earthly life taking on the identity of God's Kingdom doesn't sound like very good news. If you're a single mom trying to eke out a living for you and your kids on minimum wage, you may not welcome a continuation of this world. If you are a sex slave trapped in a brothel in India, the last thing you want is more of the same that lasts forever.

Let's not lose sight of heaven's crashing into earth and creating a very different existence from the creation we currently inhabit. In fact, you have tasted heaven already. Maybe it was when you held a new-born baby, or when you sat around a table filled with people you would give your life for, or when you stood in front of a crowd of friends and family members and made promises to your spouse to make love for a lifetime.

But you also know this sensation is fleeting. All babies grow up into the creatures known as teenagers, and sometimes spouses and family members betray us—or we betray them. Friends often move away, putting an end to our treasured times of face-to-face sharing.

No one has to be convinced that the world, as it is, just isn't right. While there are moments when heaven and earth overlap, there also are moments when *hell* seems like a more apt word to describe the world we live in. There are days it seems that hell is definitely winning.

When we look at the rise of ISIS in the war-torn nations of Iraq and

Syria or the sex-trafficking industry, people who don't believe in God or an afterlife reach for words such as *hell*.

So did Jesus.

When Jesus spoke about hell, He referred to the town dump right outside Jerusalem. It was a place of smoke and stench, with a perpetual fire going. When He talked about the human condition, He said that what is going on inside us is a bit like the town dump.

Hell and heaven are not abstract ideas about some future reality. They are, rather, one of the best ways to talk about what we experience today. The ultimate Christian hope is not to fly off as disembodied beings to another place. Our hope is that God is going to redeem and restore this world, and you and me along with it.

We find a description of this in the last chapter of the Bible.

> Then the angel showed me the river of the water of life, as clear as crystal, flowing from the throne of God and of the Lamb down the middle of the great street of the city. On each side of the river stood the tree of life, bearing twelve crops of fruit, yielding its fruit every month. And the leaves of the tree are for the healing of the nations. No longer will there be any curse. The throne of God and of the Lamb will be in the city, and his servants will serve him. They will see his face, and his name will be on their foreheads. (Revelation 22:1–4)

If you were to read the first three chapters of Genesis, and then immediately read Revelation chapters 21 and 22, you would notice that these two books are in conversation with each other. Revelation describes the original Garden of Eden, and then in one of the best verses in the Bible, it tells us, "No longer will there be any curse" (22:3).

The reason it's so hard to wrap our minds around God's act of re-

deeming His creation is because we aren't familiar with life that is not
tainted by the curse. God has no plans to perpetuate the broken world we
live in. Instead, He will reclaim His good creation and reverse the curse.

Have you noticed that the Bible doesn't talk much about the Fall?
The Old Testament doesn't even refer to what Adam and Eve did in the
garden when they defied God's one prohibition. When we do see the
Garden of Eden referred to after Genesis 3, it almost always is cast in a
positive way. It's about how the garden will one day be restored.

This is why, in ancient times, the people of God never thought of
God's judgment as a bad thing. In modern times, Westerners have
thought in terms of God judging individuals, and while that is an aspect
of God's judgment, it has never been the main point.

The main point of God's judgment is that He will reverse the curse:
He will place His judgment on death in all its forms. In Revelation, as
John described his vision, he mentioned something that is easy to miss:
"There will be no more night. They will not need the light of a lamp or
the light of the sun, for the Lord God will give them light. And they will
reign for ever and ever" (22:5).

Whenever light is mentioned in the Bible, pay close attention. It is
the first thing God created. Light exposes and reveals. When light shines
into darkness, it allows us to see what previously had been unseen.

Along with light comes a layer of judgment. There are no more se-
crets; ultimate reality is totally and finally exposed.

A More Accurate Understanding of Judgment

It has been said that the most quoted verse in the Bible is Matthew 7:1:
"Do not judge." I understand why these words of Jesus appeal to so many
people.

I have seen heinous things done in the name of religion. In the name

of their god, people have flown planes into buildings, committed genocide, and served poisoned Kool-Aid to gullible followers. Like me, I'm
sure you have seen street preachers and regular preachers alike name everything and everyone they hate, and then mention Jesus as if He endorses
their hatred. We have seen religion destroy relationships and make people
more self-focused, more violent, and more hateful.

Almost every day on social media, people ask me to like their Face-
book page or to vote for some idol or dancing star. We are accosted by
people asking us to review something at Amazon. (Obviously, we'll make
an exception for the book you are now reading. Feel free to visit Amazon.
com and review *Bringing Heaven to Earth*.)

We keep looking around to determine how we compare to others.
We keep track of our peers as we wonder who is smarter, funnier, or more
well-informed. We have been conditioned to gauge our acceptability on a
scale of one to ten.

We judge people all the time, as if we were living in a beauty pageant.
This is far from what God desires for us. N. T. Wright has pointed out:

> For God to judge the world meant that he would, in the end, put
> it all to rights, straighten it out, producing not just a sigh of relief
> all around but shouting for joy from the trees and the fields, the
> seas and the floods.[3]

GOD'S PRESENCE IS THE JUDGMENT

The prophet Isaiah was given a glimpse into the heavens (see Isaiah
6:1–3). He had a brush with God's glory, which sounds wonderful.
But when Isaiah saw God, he felt exposed. The experience humbled
him, even though God didn't say a word about what was wrong with

this outspoken prophet. But by God's very presence, Isaiah was undone.

Think about the Gospel accounts that describe Jesus's first encounters with the men who would become His disciples (see Luke 5:4–9). In one such account, fishermen had spent the night on the water and were coming back empty-handed. Jesus helped them catch an abundance of fish, and Peter immediately fell down and said, "Go away from me Lord; I am a sinful man!" (Luke 5:8).

Jesus has said nothing about how sinful Peter was. But by His mere presence, Peter was convicted. God's presence causes us to recognize that something is off inside of us. When God appears, we become intensely aware of where we fall short. No one sees God and then says, "Yeah . . . but you should see my friend Gary. He's *really* messed up."

In *The Magician's Nephew* by C. S. Lewis, a boy named Digory set an evil witch loose on the freshly created land of Narnia. The witch had been imprisoned by a curse that she had used to spite her sister and destroy her world. The only thing that could free the witch was the ringing of a bell. Digory stumbled into her world, and his curiosity overwhelmed him.

Of course, he rang the bell, freeing the witch. He reasoned that he would have gone mad with curiosity if he hadn't rung the bell. Anyway, he had no idea that evil would come about as a result.

Such justifications made it possible for Digory to sleep at night, until the boy met Aslan. In the presence of Aslan, Digory couldn't hide. At first he told Aslan that he believed he must have been under the witch's enchantment when he rang the bell. But Aslan pressed in:

> "Do you [really believe that]?" asked Aslan; still speaking very low and deep.
>
> "No," said Digory, "I see now. . . . I was only pretending."[4]

The light, God's presence, reveals us, exposing all the ways we have been pretending. But it does more than just expose. The light also heals.

In Genesis, we are told that we were made in the image of God. Theologians call this the *Imago Dei,* and if you believe in human rights or the idea that all people everywhere are equal, you are in line with one aspect of this truth.

The idea of inherent human value is connected to a story about how people are connected to God. When God reveals Himself, something inside us comes alive. That aliveness reminds us of what we were created to be, while it also exposes cracks in our soul.

This is what it means for God's light to shine into darkness. This is, in part, how God judges. When He shows up, His presence exposes what is wrong. And what needs to be healed and redeemed.

The Forgotten, Judgmental Jesus

In the Gospel of Matthew we find Jesus telling back-to-back stories about God's judgment. In the first, He makes it clear to His disciples that no one but the Father knows the day or the time of the Age to Come. The second story has to do with a master who, before setting off on a journey, entrusted three servants with what amounted to a fortune, telling them make some investments while he was away (see Matthew 25:14–30). The third has to do with separating people into the categories of sheep and goats (see Matthew 25:31–46).

Let's look first at the servants who were told to become investors.

Three servants making investment decisions

A man who had three servants was about to leave town. He called the servants together and gave them each a portion of his estate to steward and invest. One servant received five talents, another got two talents, and the last guy got only one.

Masters often would go away and entrust servants with the care of their estate. We know this is a very trusting master, because he gave three servants a lot of money. A talent was worth ten years' wages, anywhere from $250,000 to $1 million. This amount of money in cash would have weighed around seventy-five pounds. We might feel bad for the one-talent guy, but even one talent was nothing to gloss over. This master is the Warren Buffet of ancient times.

The servants, who now were wealth managers, previously had been nobodies. This was not just an investment of money—this was an investment in the lives of three people. And everything hinged on what they would do with the opportunity.

Would all three invest wisely? Would one or more of them squander the riches? What would be the outcome of this story?

The servants lived in an honor-shame culture. If they failed at this assignment, it might ruin their lives. That might explain why the one-talent guy responded the way he did. He found a nice hole in the ground, buried his bag of loot, and walked away. He played it safe without realizing that was the most dangerous move of all.

Think again about the story as Jesus told it. Two of the servants doubled the amount that was entrusted to them. The second guy showed less than half the return of the first guy, but the master told them both, "Well done" (Matthew 25:21).

This is not a story about God wanting maximum production; it's about God wanting partners. Notice the next thing the master said to the first two servants: "Come and share your master's happiness!" (Matthew 25:23). Their reward wasn't a comfortable retirement; instead it was that they got to continue partnering with their master.

Jesus, judgment, sheep, and goats

Another of Jesus's stories that talks about judgment has to do with His separating people into the categories of sheep and goats.

I (Jonathan) grew up on a farm where sheep and goats were abundant, so this parable makes sense to me. It's not that one animal is better than the other. Sheep are some of the dumbest animals in the world, but they do tend to obey better than goats. Goats, in my experience, are the most cynical animals in the world. They are the Nietzsches of the animal kingdom.

Jesus talked about separating sheep from goats, but the particulars weren't what His listeners expected. According to Jesus, some people who were convinced they knew Him were out, while others who thought they didn't know Him were in.

In all of this talk about judgment, there is no mention of the earth's burning up. (We often are asked about this.) It is not that the world will be destroyed in fire, but more that all will be found out.[5] Some of us will be surprised, as we see in the outcome of the sheep-and-goats story. The refining process of judgment goes straight to the heart of each person—whether goat or sheep.

Throughout Scripture, God's judgment is seen as a good thing. When you are vulnerable to the whims of kings and princes who seem to run this world, it's good to know there is Someone who holds rulers accountable. But there's more. From the Hebrew prophets to the New Testament, the idea of a future judgment was always presented as a reminder for how to live *in the present*.

This is personal for each of us. When heaven crashes into earth, judgment will reveal what I have done with my life. I'm a sheep or a goat. I would argue that most of us have an intuition about this: we know what is really worthwhile in life. There are things that matter and things that don't.

It's possible to be a Christian and still waste your life. In fact, many Christians are doing just that. But Jesus wants us to be the kind of people who help to bring heaven to earth. That means, among other things, that we will pursue justice in our careers and in life. It means being aware of others and the condition of the world, and living intentionally. Checking our contacts list to see if our circle of friends is too limited (meaning too homogenous). Asking the hard questions about how we use our money, our time, and our influence to combat greed and racism, and to serve our neighbors.

The stuff that we do that is in line with God's new creation will last, and that which isn't will be burned away. The church is called to live and work in this world that is already being made new!

YOU CAN'T FAKE FRENCH

I (Jonathan) was homeschooled. I imagine all kinds of stereotypes are coming to your mind right now. Pick one: Duggar family, *I Kissed Dating Goodbye,* Amish farm boy driving a buggy. But my experience had little in common with any of that. My mom was my teacher, and she wanted me to learn a foreign language. She didn't know a language other than English, so she ordered a tape curriculum designed to teach French to a fifth grader.

This was pre–Rosetta Stone (the company, not the actual stone), and the curriculum wasn't all that helpful. If you've ever had to learn a foreign language on your own, you know how difficult it can be.

It dawned on me that since I was the only one learning the language, I was the only one who could tell if I was learning it. It's kind of like today when people ask if I know Greek, I immediately ask them, "Do you?" If they don't, then I'm an expert.

I could just fast-forward the tape on my French lessons. My mom had no idea if I had done the work of learning the vocabulary, or if I had simply pressed a button on the tape player. How could she review me?

I went ahead and learned a few French sentences to impress her. Or I should say they were French-ish. I can still remember one. It was *Le pois-son est dans le bain*. Roughly translated it means "The fish is in the bath."

Le poisson est dans le bain.

Ah. French truly is the language of love.

This worked well for me until the day when my mom and I were at a yard sale held by a woman who grew up in Paris. Eager to show off her son's acquisition of a second language, my mom introduced me and explained that I had been taking French. Suddenly, it was the Day of the *Lord*.

I don't care how many ways you try to conjugate a sentence about a fish in a bathtub, it eventually will fall apart. In my case, it also left in its wake a confused French woman and a very angry mother.

I was, how do you say, *"Le grounded."*

This leads to my making a point about religion and heaven and our ideas about the afterlife. We focus on whether we'll get into heaven, but that's not the issue. We would do better to understand the nature of heaven and what bearing it has on the life of God's people on earth.

Usually when Christians talk about heaven, the discussion becomes either abstract or exclusionary. The conversation turns to streets of gold and gates of pearl, or the talk soon turns to who's in and who's out.

I think God will be more generous than any of us imagine. That's much of the meaning of mercy. None of us deserves it, yet all of us are in desperate need of it. Keep in mind the sheep-and-goats story. You might be convinced you're a sheep, and you might find out it's better to be a goat. You and I will be surprised when we run into certain people in heaven. Some people will be surprised to see *you* there!

Here is what the gospel points us to: the world one day is going to be set right. What Jesus accomplished through His death, burial, and resurrection reversed the curse of the Fall.

Those of us who have learned how to follow Jesus well will be fluent in the language of God. Do you suppose it would have changed the way

I studied French if I had known in advance that one day I would want to propose to my girlfriend while in Paris?

I'm confident that I would have been more diligent in my study of French back in fifth grade. Not for the grade, but for practice. Psychologists refer to this idea as an intrinsic reward.

You might spend your life discriminating against people who aren't like you, but when heaven crashes into earth, there will be people from every tribe and every tongue in God's Kingdom. You might not like it that much living next door to someone who, during your lifetime, you treated as your inferior.

Remember the older brother in the parable of the prodigal son? He was upset that his father gave grace when the older brother felt it was not deserved. The dutiful older brother felt that, because of his years of slaving, he deserved his father's grace. But the ungrateful, hedonistic younger brother? No way!

This parable was first told to moral insiders, the same type of people who today are named as elders, preachers, and ministry leaders. It is significant that the older brother mentioned that for years he had been *slaving*. The word would have brought to mind a time in Jewish history, one they reenacted and rehearsed every year at Passover, reflecting on their enslavement in Egypt.

In telling this story, Jesus was gently reminding the moral insiders that God isn't like Pharaoh. God is no slave driver; He is a good and generous Father. The parable is fair warning to us as well, helping us recognize how religion can blind us. Over years and years of service, we start to forget how good God has been to us.

Jesus was reminding religious leaders of the heart of God and the plans of God. When heaven crashes into earth, we will discover there is a center of the universe . . . but it isn't you or me.

Jesus gave us a picture of the way the world is going to be one day, so go ahead and start practicing now. It's not a bad thing for our works to be exposed, because the God who does the judging is very good.

Some of you have quietly served and loved people, and you have no idea how much of an impact you've made. You didn't know that when you invited a college student to lunch, she learned that she mattered. You had no idea that a word of encouragement you gave to an acquaintance kept him from ending his life. You didn't realize that your generosity kept someone alive.

God promises He will restore all things, and what we have done with our lives will be exposed. For some that will be painful. For others it will be wonderful. For many it will be both. We are to live on earth as if we already are living in heaven. When heaven crashes into earth, you and I can already be fluent in the language that is being spoken there. And that is the language of love and restoration.

Many of the ideas in this chapter were inspired by the work of theologian Dallas Willard. As he lay dying in 2013, it became evident that this was reality to him, not just a set of interesting ideas.

As he approached death, Dallas Willard said, "I think that when I die, it might be some time until I know it."[6]

In his book *Soul Keeping,* John Ortberg described the way Dallas Willard died. He quoted Gary Black, a friend of the theologian: "It's like a conversation with a person who is about to cross over into a room that you cannot see and where you cannot go." Gary reported that even in the midst of intense pain, Dallas Willard's final words were, "Thank you. Thank you." In his book, Ortberg pointed out that "Dallas wasn't talking to Gary."

Gary recalled that the phrase that came to mind, as he watched Dallas walk in the valley of the shadow of death, was "Game on." Death had met its match.[7]

When the Day of the Lord arrives, what we've done with our lives that has been in tune with God's new creation will last forever.

A Marriage Made in Heaven

God Gives Himself to Us Like an Eager Groom

> The kingdom of heaven is like a king who
> prepared a wedding banquet for his son.
>
> — Jesus (Matthew 22:2)

> Mawwiage. Mawwiage is what bwings us
> togethaw today. Mawwiage, that bwessed
> awwangement, that dweam within a dweam.
>
> — Officiating clergyman in
> *The Princess Bride*

For several years, I (Jonathan) was a church singles minister. I have performed in the neighborhood of one hundred weddings. It's one of my favorite parts of ministry, and every time I witness a wedding, hundreds of verses in the Bible start to make more sense. God's covenants in the Old Testament and the wedding stories in the New Testament come into sharper focus.

At a wedding, people who rarely pause to think about God stop and watch a modern-day parable.

What We Can Learn from Weddings

Recently I got to officiate at my friend Darryl's wedding. Darryl is a brand-new Christian and has a life that is different from mine. We both grew up poor, but as an African American male, Darryl's poverty took a different shape.

He was abused and neglected as a child, and later he was imprisoned for some bad choices he made. For a decade before we met, Darryl had taken to cutting himself to help him deal with the swirling chaos inside him. Through a series of coincidences, he and I met. After getting to know the Jesus story, Darryl was baptized and welcomed to the church family.

Darryl and I had become friends, and he asked if I would perform the wedding for him and Betty. They'd lived with each other for a few years, and he wanted to "put a ring on it." Betty had a pretty demanding job, so we planned to have the wedding rehearsal right before the wedding. Unfortunately, the wedding party didn't show up until five minutes before the ceremony was scheduled to begin. Okay, it was half the wedding party.

Those numbered among the half that *did* show up weren't show ready. The bride and groom arrived wearing sandals and shorts. They changed into dresses and suits in a church bathroom while friends and family and church family waited in the sanctuary.

Once everyone was dressed, we faced another wave of difficulties. Turns out one of the groomsmen that showed up wasn't feeling well. He had a severe headache, finding relief by pacing around the sanctuary swearing.

I decided to get the show on the road. To achieve symmetry in the bridal party, I pulled a college student out of the audience to be a stand-in groomsman. We started the solemn ceremony.

At least it was meant to be solemn.

It seemed like everyone was up moving around, talking, and taking pictures. Some of the guests got on the stage behind me to take pictures with their phones. In the middle of the recessional, Captain Headache came back up to the front. By then he was carrying a two-year-old. The groomsman tried to hand the kid off to a bridesmaid.

But the bridesmaid refused to take the handoff. What followed was a kind of reverse tug-of-war over a toddler. You take her, no you keep her . . . Finally, the bridesmaid took the kid and walked down the aisle with a replacement groomsman on one arm and the child in the other.

I found out later that one bridesmaid was a sex worker, and this was the first time in years that she had been inside a church. At some point, this woman had decided that the best shot she had to achieve a measure of happiness was to sell her body.

Right after the wedding, she whispered to me, "I wish I could get married one day."

Buried in this wish is more than just a hope for a ceremony. It is the question that haunts each of us. It drives us to work too many hours or to drink too much or to find ourselves in a stranger's bed. It is the question, "Does anyone . . . will anyone ever . . . really love me?"

A Thirsty God

This is what all of humanity is thirsty for, to love and to be loved.

The Gospel of John is different from the other three, which open with stories about Jesus's baptism and temptation. In contrast, John opens by telling us about Jesus at a wedding (see John 2:1–10). It was the scene of His first miracle; He turned water into wine. Jesus quenched the thirst that the people had, not just for wine, but for a moment when all was right in the world.

This story is a big deal to John. He opened his Gospel with Jesus giving people wine, and he closed it by telling how deeply Jesus shared in the suffering of the world. Jesus did not just bear the violence of a Roman cross. We read in John's Gospel that Jesus was dying because He was thirsty.

At the end of the Gospel of John, we read that John didn't tell us everything. He wrote down only what would help people have faith in Jesus. If he had tried to write everything, there wouldn't be enough books in the world to hold it. Given the fact that John concentrated on the essential stuff, it's significant that his is the only Gospel that opens with Jesus at a wedding.

He referred to it as a sign.

Weddings are a sign. When the prophets and disciples and Jesus talked about heaven, the talk was of parties and wine and banquets and weddings. But for some reason, that imagery has not gotten across to most of us. If you were to stop someone on the street and ask her what she thought heaven was like, I doubt she would say, "It's a lot like a wedding."

But God introduced marriage very close to the beginning of the world. God created Adam and breathed into the man the breath of life. Then God created Eve, someone equal to the man, in order to share life with him.

When God gave the first woman to the first man, the world saw its first wedding. And it was performed by God.

When Adam first saw Eve, he broke out into poetry. He declared her to be bone of his bone and flesh of his flesh (see Genesis 2:23). *Bone* is a Hebrew metaphor for strength, and *flesh* is one for weakness. Adam was saying, "Where I am weak, Eve is strong. Where Eve is weak, I am strong." They were different, unique, and made for each other.

After the Fall, Adam and Eve were no longer enamored of how well they complemented each other. They fell quickly into mutual blame. Later, one of their sons introduced death and murder into the world. When the dust cleared, the only thing still standing was their marriage.

And in every generation since, marriage has held special importance for God's people. Catholics consider a wedding to be a sacrament. Marriage is a calling that taps into the deepest realities and gives the world a glimpse of what God is like. Sacraments are a way God says something about Himself to the world.

Maybe that's why the Bible talks so much about marriage, and why Paul ended so many of his letters talking about marriage. A marriage is more than two people making promises; it is two people making parables, committing to show with their lives the way God loves the world.[1]

When a marriage is at its best, when a husband is giving himself fully to his wife and she is giving herself fully to him, they aren't trying to define themselves as better than the other. They don't try to justify their own behavior. In spite of their differences, they try to reconcile for the sake of the gospel.

I have preached so many funerals where the husband or wife was saying good-bye to a spouse, and the whole church was moved. I've seen a tangible change in the atmosphere when the church gathers to mourn a person who died, leaving behind his or her spouse. They are celebrating the faithfulness of these two people.

When a marriage goes the distance, it is a glimpse of the gospel. It's something that is hard to explain, even harder to live, but easy to understand when you see it.

In marriage, we are forced to reconcile what previously had been separated. And this is a major reason why marriages in the church matter for all of us, whether we are married or not. Paul wrote about husbands and wives because everyone needed to hear this message (see Ephesians 5:21–33). Marriages are a way God reminds His people of the kind of community He is creating. We are being reconciled to the same God, so we each have to make room for one another.

Overlooked Wedding Invitations

The Bible refers to weddings and marriage in ways that we often over-look—or just don't get. In the book of Exodus, God calls the Israelites to Mount Sinai. He had just freed them from slavery to be His priests to the world. To help the Hebrews do this, God gave them the Torah.

Most of us hear *Torah* and think "law." But to say the Torah is just the Law is like saying the Cross is wood. It's a lot more than that.

When the Israelites first received the Law, they were ecstatic. They had lived in slavery for more than four hundred years. All they had known was life as an oppressed people. So their sojourn in the wilderness was a transition period from slavery to occupying the land God was about to give them. If God had set them free in the desert without adequate preparation, it would have been a disaster.

For the Israelites, the law was grace. God was showing them the best possible way to live. Look at what God told them just before giving them the Law: "I am the LORD your God." (Exodus 6:7).

The Law wasn't a condition of the relationship; it was a confirmation of it. In fact, the language that is used, "I have brought you out, I will make you a treasured possession" (see Exodus 19:5), is wedding language. The former slaves would recognize it the way you recognize lines such as "Do you promise to have and to hold, for better or for worse?"

To this day, Jews get married under a *chuppah* (a tapestry), which represents the cloud of God that led the Israelites out of Egypt. God is proposing to Israel, and the people say, "I do." This helps make sense of the way the prophets talked about God, who often is described in Scripture as being jealous. Unlike other gods, this God has a heart, and we belong to Him. In some mysterious way, He allows Himself to belong to us.

In other words, God married His people.

Throughout the Bible, God makes promises that one day He will set the world right. He will do away with death and poverty and violence and will make everything the way He always intended for it to be. This explains scenes such as Isaiah 25 or 65, where we see vivid pictures of what a world set right will look like.

God will rejoice over His people, and they will rejoice with Him. Lions will lie down with lambs. Heaven is pledged to earth.

WEDDINGS NEED WINE

In Jesus's day, most weddings were arrangements between the families involved. After two people were engaged, the groom had to go prepare a place where the couple would live. Most of the time this consisted of an add-on to the father's estate.

During this year of preparation, the bride would learn from her mother what it meant to be a good wife. When the groom had finished building their home, the father would inspect it, and when he had approved, the groom and his friends would begin their wedding parade to go get his bride.[2]

In Jesus's day, the wedding parade was a widely known symbol of the Kingdom of God. A bride knew that getting married involved waiting for the one she loved to come back.

In Matthew 25, Jesus tells a story of the wise and foolish virgins. (Coincidentally, this also was the name of my homeschool basketball team.) In the story, ten virgins wait for a wedding parade. They know approximately the time that the wedding is supposed to take place, but not exactly. Eventually half of them run out of oil. Around midnight they leave to obtain oil for their lamps, and while they are gone, the groom arrives.

I grew up reading that story as one of judgment, a word of caution, saying we should be prepared for Jesus's return. On one level that's what the story tells us. But when Jesus first told the story, the people would have laughed. Midnight wedding parades were rare.[3] To be sure, the message of the story is that you never know when Jesus might return, so be prepared. But another layer of this story is that a midnight wedding parade indicates that the groom simply could wait no longer. To explain the Kingdom of God, Jesus told about a wedding parade involving a man who was so madly in love he showed up at midnight.

This helps us appreciate why the Gospel of John opens with a wedding. It was a time of celebration, but the host ran out of wine. This was an honor/shame culture in which the worst thing possible was to lose face in a social setting. Running out of wine was a tragedy.

In the Jewish world, a wedding would last up to a week. Weddings weren't like other parties; they were a parable of what would happen when God finally returned to set the world right. Once again God would wed heaven to earth, which is why weddings were considered the thin space where heaven and earth got just a bit closer.

The Jewish people were critical of excessive drinking, except at weddings. At wedding feasts it seemed that an entire culture was given permission to celebrate without limits.[4] The host was expected to provide wine for the community during a wedding celebration, and to do that the host would have saved up for years.

Wine was a luxury that the poor didn't have ready access to—except at weddings. This helps explain why Mary came to Jesus to see if He might help out. It's here that she cashed in her chips from that whole giving-birth-to-Jesus-in-a-barn ordeal.

Jesus initially told her no, and just like my mom she ignored His response and got Him some volunteers. Jesus pointed them toward stone jars used for cleaning hands, in a culture where hands could get really dirty, really fast. He had the volunteers fill the jars with water. Then He told them to take the dirty water to the master of the banquet to have him taste it. We tend to read over this as if it were normal. But this water wasn't meant for drinking. The waiters were basically asking the boss to drink waste water.

But the master of the banquet discovered that the jars contained really good wine. He called the groom and bride over and told them, unlike the other wedding parties he had attended, that they had saved the best wine for last. As if John is letting us know that Jesus throws the best parties. He always makes the party better.

John wrote that the miracle at the wedding feast was a sign, one of the seven that Jesus gives in the Gospel of John. Further, there are seven days of creation. John begins his gospel with the words "In the beginning." This echoes the creation account in Genesis.

After the crucifixion, similar to the seventh day of creation, God rested in the tomb. John made it clear that Jesus's resurrection is about more than just one Man rising from the dead. This has something to do with the creation project that God has been working on all along. John wanted us to see that Jesus's resurrection has to do with a new creation.

Jesus opened His ministry to save a broken and hurting humanity by affirming and celebrating the very heart of humanity. He performed His first miracle at a party with wine, friends, and a good wedding. It is for good reason you can't turn on a radio without hearing a song about love. Romantic love for many is the end itself; it is unquestionably a great idol of our day. But dreamy fantasies about romance fail to grasp how significant love really is.

Whenever someone tells me that God told her to marry this particular person, I am skeptical. But whatever gave me that impulse when I first met my wife, Leslie, I thank God for. The moment she walked into the room, suddenly it was as though I had been color blind, but that in a single moment, I was given the whole spectrum of color.

In fact, framed in our house above our fireplace is this commitment I wrote down that very night:

I wrote that I was going to marry Leslie. I even misspelled her name. On some level, I have always been a romantic person. But romantic love is never the end in itself; it always points past itself. It progresses; it forces us to make promises and ultimately to give ourselves away. It progresses, a lot of times, to a wedding.

We find in weddings two distinct people becoming one. That is why God uses a wedding as a sign for a future reality.

Then I saw "a new heaven and a new earth," for the first heaven
and the first earth had passed away, and there was no longer any
sea. I saw the Holy City, the new Jerusalem, coming down out
of heaven from God, prepared as a bride beautifully dressed for

her husband. And I heard a loud voice from the throne saying, "Look! God's dwelling place is now among the people, and he will dwell with them. They will be his people, and God himself will be with them and be their God. 'He will wipe every tear from their eyes. There will be no more death' or mourning or crying or pain, for the old order of things has passed away." (Revelation 21:1–4)

God has been telling a story about Himself and about us for a very long time. He ends the telling of the story not with an earthquake or fire, not with destruction, *but with a wedding.* Heaven comes down, and earth and heaven are one.

N. T. Wright has written about this passage:

Heaven and earth, it seems, are not after all poles apart, needing to be separated forever when all the children of heaven have been rescued from this wicked earth. Nor are they simply different ways of looking at the same thing . . . No, they are different, radically different, but they are made for each other in the same way (Revelation is suggesting) as male and female. And when they finally come together, that will be cause for rejoicing in the same way that a wedding is: a creational sign that God's project is going forward; that opposite poles within creation are made for union, not competition; that love and not hate have the last word in the universe; that fruitfulness and not sterility is God's will for creation.[5]

God will do for the world what He did for Jesus. God will restore all things; He will bring heaven and earth together fully and finally. And the coming together looks a lot like a wedding.

WEDDINGS ARE GOSPEL PRODUCTIONS

When it comes to weddings and funerals, the church is where a lot of people turn for help. The church is called to help, so the beginning of this story is great. But I have seen pastors try to turn weddings into manipulative gospel presentations. What they are missing is that the wedding itself is a gospel production. So why not stop talking about the gospel and, instead, put it on display?

I tell every bridal party that I love doing weddings almost more than anything else in ministry. Every wedding is a parable, a picture of who God is and what He is doing in the world. I love weddings because Jesus loved weddings.

I know that many individuals in a wedding party are not religious, and they may not know what they think about God. But as part of a wedding ceremony, they are participating in a parable about the heart of God. Romance helps us to tap into a deep vein of who God is. That's why John opens his gospel with a wedding. Weddings celebrate what happens when love must move forward.

Because God so loves the world.

Romantic love for many is the end itself, but that fails to grasp how big it actually is. This is how C. S. Lewis expressed it:

> The Event of falling in love is of such a nature that we are right to
> reject as intolerable the idea that it should be transitory. In one
> high bound it has overleaped the massive wall of our selfhood; it
> has made appetite itself altruistic, tossed personal happiness aside
> as a triviality and planted the interest of another in the centre of
> our being. Spontaneously and without effort we have fulfilled the
> law (towards one person) by loving our neighbor as ourselves. It is

an image, a foretaste, of what we must become to all if Love Himself rules in us without a rival. It is even . . . preparation for that.[6]

William Shakespeare said in *The Tempest* about lovers, "They have chang'd eyes." And he was right. For a brief time, romance gives us the ability to see the best in one other person. We are able to ignore their flaws, and they are able to ignore ours.

This gives us a glimpse into how we will view every resurrected person, and most of all, God. This is what every wedding promises, but no marriage can fully deliver. It is a glimpse into the heart of God and the purposes of God for the world.

Several years ago, I was having breakfast with a friend named Mike. He is an older Jewish man who had come to believe that Jesus was the Messiah. Toward the end of the conversation, I asked him to explain the Jewish concept of heaven.

He told me that the previous year his mother had been on her deathbed in Florida, and he went to say good-bye. As he was holding her hand, she sat up and stared past him, saying, "Can you see it? That's beautiful."

These were the last words she said on this side of mystery. A few hours later she passed away. Mike told this story at his mother's funeral, after which an older Jewish man came up to him and asked if he could tell his own story. The other man had been married to his wife for many years when she started showing signs of Alzheimer's. She suffered with it for many years, and eventually he had to put his wife in a nursing home. He explained that every day when he went to see her, he would break down. It was so difficult to see the woman he loved becoming only a shell of her former self.

Eventually she couldn't remember his name, her name, their first kiss, how he had proposed, or all the years they had spent making a life together. Now she looked at him with the blank stare you give strangers.

It was like a nightmare.

Then one day he went into her room and she opened her eyes. She remembered everything. Her name, who her husband was, how they met, their first kiss. She remembered it all.

The man said he praised God, thinking that God was giving his wife back to him. The next day his wife died. The bereaved husband said he realized what had happened. God was not giving a wife back to her husband; he was giving her back to Himself. God allowed the man to see what that was going to look like.

For God so loves the world, and every wedding points to the day when He gives us all back to Himself. To live happily ever after.

Part 2

When Heaven Celebrates

I like to picture Jesus in a tuxedo T-Shirt
because it says I want to be formal, but I'm
here to party.

— Cal Naughton Jr. in *Talladega Nights*

[Why] are you so dull?

— Jesus (Mark 7:18)

A few years ago, I (Josh) spoke at a large event for teenagers. The young people had gathered in Gatlinburg, Tennessee, for a weekend of praise. The first thing I said from the stage was "Is it just me, or does this feel like a big Jesus party?"

The next week, I heard about it. A few people weren't happy that I had used the words *Jesus* and *party* next to each other. But why?

If you can read one of the Gospels without getting hungry, you're not paying attention. Jesus is always going to or coming from a party. He's always eating, and He is frequently in trouble with the religious establishment over the people He partied with and how much He was partying.

In fact, much of the New Testament begins to make sense when we realize how different the early Christian gatherings are from what we think of today. Nearly two thousand years ago, every Sunday was called a mini-Easter by the early Christians. They would gather to share their resources, break bread, and have a party. Everyone was welcome, and the meal was both free and cost you everything.

But today, Jesus-followers have a different kind of reputation.

Most people in the West picture Christians in a way that still resembles the Puritans, who, as H. L. Mencken described, had a "haunting fear that somebody, somewhere, may be happy."

That is not an accurate picture if you are trying to faithfully follow Jesus. "The Son of Man came eating and drinking, and you say, 'Here is a glutton and a drunkard, a friend of tax collectors and sinners'" (Luke 7:34). Parties were what set Jesus apart. We tend to think religious people need to be otherworldly and ethereal, but Jesus partied like this world mattered.[1]

Here's a quick quiz. Who said, "Party or die?" The first names that come to mind might be Charlie Sheen, Miley Cyrus, or Nicki Minaj. The correct answer: God.

The book of Leviticus is far more than just the cemetery where your Read-the-Bible-in-a-Year plan goes to die. Buried among the rules for how to kill a goat and sobering lists of abominations is a life-changing, life-affirming idea. Are you ready? God commands His people to party.

God gave Israel seasons for feasting and times to be grateful for the gift of life. He asked them to set aside a portion of their income to finance parties worthy of the name. And how about us? He has given us more than enough reason to celebrate. God insists that we drop the question "What don't I have?" for better ones: "Why do I have so much? Why has God been so good to me?"

God knows a lot of us are not inclined to party. We haven't had enough practice, at least with Jesus parties. Those are the ones that do not exclude certain people. Jesus parties take into account grief, sorrow, disappointment. In fact, people going through hard times have always been high on Jesus's guest list.

If we have any hope of joining Jesus in His Kingdom work on earth, we have to learn how to party. Jesus specialized in gathering all the wrong people in all the wrong places. He would gather in the hated tax collectors and the shamed prostitutes to the table, break some bread and say, "This is what heaven is like."

7

Guilty Parties

God Uses Restored People to Restore People

> All these years I've been slaving.
> — The older brother (Luke 15:29)

> Why are you so angry?
> — God to Jonah (see Jonah 4:4)

Bob Goff is a well-known author, speaker, and attorney. He's a man who lives every moment intentionally. In a talk I heard him give, he said he often invites people who don't know him well to come to his home for dinner. One of the first questions people ask is, Who else will be there?

You might recall that such a concern is common among students, when a kid is trying to decide whether to attend a party or go to a dance. But questions about the guest list aren't limited to insecure adolescents. The concerns might even intensify the older we get and the more broken we become.

Think about what happened in the church when people such as Saul, the former persecutor of Christians; Zacchaeus, an unethical tax collector; and various wanton women (including prostitutes) began receiving invitations to Kingdom parties. I'm not sure which question caused more tension for faith communities: "Who invited them?" or "Did God invite *them*?"

Let's dive into a conversation about our hearts, relationships, and justice.

THE PRODIGAL SONS

The prodigal son story ranks as one of the most well-known stories in the New Testament (see Luke 15). It is a parable told by Jesus—a fictional story—yet it represents a situation that happens all the time, even today.

Jesus told the story to religious people who had taken offense at Jesus for the way He ministered to people. They also objected to the people who were receiving His help and attention. The critics felt that Jesus spent too much time with sinners. So Jesus told them a story about two sons and a dad. The younger son went off and blew his inheritance on the same things that most young men blow their money on.

After the younger son hit rock bottom, he decided to return home. The entire way back he worked on his apology to his father. When you have blown it as badly as he had, you need a pretty impressive apology. The young man had decided he would work like a slave for his dad. If he could just get a few meals and a roof over his head, he would take whatever job his father would offer.

The father had been hoping and waiting for his son's return. He spotted the son even when he was far off, and the father ran to meet the young man. The father didn't even let his son finish his prepared apology before he went into party planning mode. They threw a party with music and dancing, and they roasted a calf. Then the dad noticed that his older son had gone prodigal.

Like before, the dad who always was watching out for his boys went to the other son and tried to get him to join the party. God does this all the time. He tries to get us all to join in His mission for the world.

The older son, however, was angry. He told his dad, "You've done all these great things for my worthless brother, but what about me? I've always stayed in line; I've never done anything as blatantly stupid as my brother did. My entire life I've worked for you tirelessly."

However, those are not the words he used. What he said is this: "All these years I've been slaving for you" (verse 29). *Slavery* is a word that would have caught the attention of the religious leaders who made up Jesus's audience. The nation of Israel began in slavery. The Hebrews made bricks for Pharaoh, a master who had no compassion. They were given a production quota that could never be satisfied. The older brother in Jesus's parable thought he was that type of slave.

This story is painful, because the father of the two brothers is nothing like Pharaoh. He said to his elder son: "Everything I have belongs to you. I'm not your slavemaster. I'm your dad" (see verse 31).

It didn't matter to the older son what the reality was. If you see your father as a Pharaoh, then chances are you are going to see yourself as a slave. You then will view your work as a way to earn something that was yours all along.

This story was told more than two thousand years ago, but it speaks to our age better than any story I know. When most of us think of sloth, we think of laziness. But it's more than that. It's a failure to properly name the world and our place in it. It's calling something slavery instead of seeing that it is working for the Father.

Here is Dorothy Sayers's definition of *sloth:*

It is the sin which believes in nothing, cares for nothing, seeks to know nothing, interferes with nothing, enjoys nothing, loves nothing, hates nothing, finds purpose in nothing, lives for nothing, and only remains alive because there is nothing it would die for. We have known it far too well for many years. The only thing perhaps we have not known about it is it is a mortal sin. . . . In the world it calls itself Tolerance; but in hell it is called Despair.[1]

Americans are addicted to work. From 1968 to 1988, the average American added one hundred sixty-three hours to his annual workload.[2] That's a month of work! So maybe it shouldn't come as a shock that we don't know how to play or to party. All we know is how to work. And more often than not, it is not a good work ethic—it's sloth.

We work long hours to avoid the hard work that needs to be done in our relationships, or the hard work of being a parent or a spouse. Too often we use work as a way to avoid life, but God intends that we use work as a way to engage life *with Him*.

Ask yourself whom you are working for. In the prodigal son story, Jesus was pleading with religious leaders. He was talking to the moral insiders—the good people. The older brother is dutiful, loyal, diligent, conscientious. He was the type of person who, today, would chair a committee or lead a ministry. Yet he was upset with the Father's goodness shown to people who, in his mind, didn't deserve it.

Too often, people who are willing to spend their lives slaving for the Lord are those most likely to forget the nature of the Lord. Grace, mercy, goodness, forgiveness. Those can be especially hard for someone who views herself as God's slave.

WHAT'S SO DIFFICULT ABOUT GRACE?

No one has a problem with grace in theory; it's the particulars that trip us up. When grace calls you to be patient and understanding toward a person who wronged you or who doesn't see the world the way you do, it's a different story.

Fred was passionate about justice, equality, and fairness. He grew up in Mississippi, observing all the ways in which African Americans were treated as second-class citizens. He decided that when he grew up, he would make a difference.

After he got his law degree, Fred became a civil rights lawyer. For two decades he fought for disenfranchised people. Eventually the NAACP gave him an award for defending the rights of African Americans in Topeka, Kansas. He risked his career and livelihood and reputation as a lawyer by taking cases that no one else would take.[3]

Fred Phelps later decided to leave the practice of law and instead to plant a church. It is the infamous Westboro Baptist Church. Phelps and his congregation eventually began picketing the graveside ceremonies of fallen American soldiers. But their most hateful expressions targeted the LGBT community. Westboro church members carry pickets that celebrate AIDS and hold signs that read "God Hates Fags." Their vitriol is not limited to soldiers and LGBT persons. Fred taught his parishioners that God hates America—including pretty much anyone who is not a part of Westboro Baptist Church.

When we hear the full story of the late Fred Phelps, we can't avoid the fact that something went horribly wrong.

Some people who have dedicated their lives to great endeavors end up being incredibly angry. I can understand why: we become like what we worship. If you find yourself constantly bitter or angry, a good question to ask is, what god am I worshiping?

Fred Phelps set out to change the world for the better. He fought for justice for people who were being denied their rights. But it's possible to do what is right in the wrong way. You can serve God while worshiping an idol.

When Phelps died, I couldn't help but notice the way the world responded. The segment of the faith community that I'm a part of, progressive Christianity, responded virtually the same as everyone else. The common sentiment was "Good riddance to an evil man!"

Obviously, it was difficult to love Fred Phelps. His life caused thousands of people deep personal injury, and at the end of his life he reaped what he sowed. Even the congregation he founded had removed him from the pastorate. (Consider that this happened even though most of the church is made up of Phelps's family members.)

One way to look at the sad ending of a man who started out with such noble intentions is to say that the hell he helped create started to envelop him. I would like to state it differently. I would tell Phelps and the people he condemned that Fred was wrong about God—and that is good news for everyone, including Fred. God does not hate anyone. He always is looking for prodigals to come home.

The tendency to condemn rather than to love has spread among Christians. It is not hard to see that certain types of sin—and those involved in such sins—are condemned with greater intensity than others. But God welcomes Fred Phelps back to the party.

Christians need to relearn the lessons of mercy. It doesn't matter if you are progressive, fundamentalist, or something else: it's wrong to just write off anyone who stands in the way of your chosen objective. We can't allow ourselves to be driven by a political theory or theological system. We must be driven by the need for reconciliation.

THE HARD WORK OF RECONCILIATION

We have to be able to reconcile with people who take a stand opposite to our own. We have to learn to live alongside people we disagree with. We need to love even someone as misguided and hurtful as Fred Phelps. But the core question is not "Does God love Fred?" The question we have to ask is this: "How does God view me in my sin?" You and I both, as much as we want to be part of God's solution to the world's hurts, also are a part of the problem.

Forgiveness is best born out of awareness of our own sin and brokenness. The people who are the most merciful are the ones who have received mercy in their most broken places. Every feast that Jesus hosts is a guilty party, because Jesus fellowships with sinners. After all, does He have any other options?

We don't earn God's favor by adhering to the right orthodoxy, nor do we earn His love by exchanging dogma and legalism for the fight for justice. Too many Christians have simply switched labels, but we haven't changed our misguided attempts to be God's favorites. We can never earn anything from God. That is older-brother thinking.

The part Fred Phelps got wrong wasn't how bad sin is. It's bad. But he missed the other part: how good God is. If the gospel is good news, it has to be good news for those who join the KKK as well as for African American civil rights workers. It has to be good news for angry and judgmental members of Westboro Baptist Church as well as for members of the communities they condemn.

The early church was not a country club made up of comfortable, middle-class, white Protestants. Remember who it was that made up the congregations of the first century. Slaves and slave owners, pacifists and military generals, zealots who sought to overthrow the Roman occupation as well as tax collectors who betrayed their people to finance the Roman occupation. It was an odd mixture of opposites, which made it even more important that it was also a community of reconciliation. That is the kind of party only God can pull off.

Not that God is okay with the evil actions of Westboro Baptist Church, or that God excuses slavery or racism or sexism or any of the other ways we demean others. God sees our sin and does not treat it lightly. However, at His core God is good.

It is natural to seek revenge against those who do evil. And if you are not a Christian, I can't imagine any reason why you wouldn't seek retribution. But I believe that Dr. King was right when he said to fight the monster with the monster's game plan is to eventually become the monster. To hate a wrongdoer and to claim God agrees with you is to accept a vengeful, hate-filled god. In your desire for revenge you become the same as the wrongdoer.

God hates the way we destroy and use each other, how we pillage creation and the people God created. He hates greed, self-righteousness, and the exploitation of the weak. God hates all things that are self-destructive and destructive to others and to His creation.

But God never hates a person. God doesn't hate Fred Phelps . . . or me . . . or you. If we believe that God hates those who openly do evil, for instance the militants in ISIS who behead journalists and capture and imprison women, we will believe God hates us too when we hit bottom.

The world does not need pure justice. A sole focus on justice eventually turns ugly. What the world needs is what humanity always has needed: grace. The world needs grace from God and grace from you as you follow Jesus. Salvation is not simply a change in a person's eternal status. It is enlistment into God's mission of reconciling the whole world.

Adelaide Pollard wrote a song in 1902 called "Have Thine Own Way." Many songs don't survive from generation to generation, but some make the leap:

Have Thine own way, Lord! Have Thine own way!
    Search me and try me, Master, today![4]

These words invite the Creator of the world to examine your heart and mine. This is a risky, dangerous request.

Pollard's song echoes Psalm 139:23–24:

Search me, God, and know my heart;
    test me and know my anxious thoughts.
See if there is any offensive way in me,
    and lead me in the way everlasting.

In 2012, I (Josh) had planned a three-day trip to Kansas City so I could put the finishing touches on my first book, *Scarred Faith*. Fortunately, I was able to turn in my manuscript weeks before I was supposed to go to Kansas City, but the trip had already been booked, so my wife encouraged me to take the three days to be alone with God.

I decided to take one prayer with me: Psalm 139:23–24. I prayed these words over and over. I sensed God saying, *Keep praying those words, because you have no clue now what you are asking for.* The next thirty-six hours were disorienting. Corners of my heart were exposed for what they were. It was as if God was performing surgery on my heart, and He was poking hard.

It wasn't until the final day that I felt I was being put back together a healthier man. Restored. Ready to reenter a world God is eager to redeem.

PUTTING THE REST IN RESTORATION

We are some of the most distracted and exhausted people who have ever walked this planet. It's extremely difficult for people to pay attention. We can sit in the same room with family and friends yet fail to connect.

There are numerous benefits to technology, but let's be honest, smart phones have helped transform us into lousy human beings.

You know the feeling of being in a meaningful conversation with someone, then the phone *dings*. You can tell the other person is no longer interested in what you are saying. You could be in the middle of confessing sin or sharing about a struggle with your spouse, yet the other person is hoping you'll break eye contact so he can steal a glance at his phone.

We are addicted to distractions, and it is killing relationships. God didn't invent coffee, 5-hour ENERGY, and Red Bull to sustain worka-holics or leisure-aholics or mobile-device-aholics. Instead, He created something called *rest*.

I (Josh) struggle with this, because I don't know how to leave work at the office. I am constantly thinking about sermons, my family, my city, hurting people, and when the Dallas Mavericks will make it back to the NBA Finals.

Mondays are supposed to be my day off, the day when I usually am emotionally drained. Kayci encourages me to stay away from my phone and my computer on Mondays, but it's never easy.

One Monday, without my knowing, Kayci hid my phone. I came into the kitchen and asked where my phone was. She pointed to her back pocket, and I could see the OtterBox peeking at me. At first, maybe because I'm a dude, I interpreted her actions flirtatiously. I thought it just might be an invitation to come and get my phone back. But she had one hand on her hip, the other in the air like a stop sign, and one eyebrow raised. It was evident we were not thinking about the same thing.

Mark Buchanan, a pastor and author, was asked about his biggest regret in life. His response was "being in a hurry." That resonated with me. Especially when our oldest child began to talk. I was traveling quite a bit, and one day he stared at Kayci's phone and proceeded to call it

Daddy, as if I lived in the phone. Most of the time when he heard my voice, it was coming out of the phone.

How can God speak into such a distracted, exhausted heart? Maybe there is so much that God would love to reveal to us about His character and His mission in the world, but we have lost the ability to listen. When this happens, both our hearts *and* the world suffer.

Psalm 23 makes an interesting word choice in this familiar verse: "He makes me lie down in green pastures." Maybe that is what God has to do. He has to *make* us lie down. He has to help us remember we aren't slaves and He's not Pharaoh. Sometimes I wonder if the reason we stay busy, distracted, and exhausted is because we aren't sure God can keep the world moving if we take our hands off of life.

For the health of our hearts and for the hope of the world, God needs us to learn to be still. God uses restored people to restore people.

JESUS AND AN INFAMOUS TRAITOR

Zacchaeus was known widely as a dishonest tax collector who conspired with the Romans. He cheated his own people for personal gain and to curry favor with those who oppressed his people. We also know that he wanted to see Jesus. His curiosity was so great that he climbed a tree to get a better look. Jesus looked up at the man in a tree and invited Himself into his home. Jesus and the cheating, disloyal tax collector had dinner and a party (see Luke 19:1–10).

It's not surprising that some of the onlookers couldn't fathom that Jesus would associate with someone so immoral. But here's where Jesus totally messes with you, with the local church, and with the way we live in the world. Jesus saw the lost and hurting as people to be pursued, not avoided.

For some, sitting in a bar with friends sounds evil. For others it sounds like what Jesus would do.

For some, crime and blight are to be avoided. For others, crime and blight need to be transformed by people who have been transformed.

Jesus pursued the encounter because He knew that changing Zacchaeus's heart would mean setting pieces of the world right as well. Jesus had a genuine concern for Zacchaeus, and He envisioned that a restored Zacchaeus would bring restoration to those Zacchaeus had harmed.

It wasn't until Zacchaeus decided to make things right with people that Jesus pronounced salvation upon his house. The point is not that he earned his salvation, but that encounters with Jesus will leave you with transformed perspectives and priorities.

Notice in the story that Jesus doesn't ask Zacchaeus to quit his job. Instead, he was told to change his attitude toward people. Was there a place in the first-century world for God-fearing, Jesus-loving, Spirit-filled tax collectors? Apparently Jesus thought so. And to change much of the world around Zacchaeus, Jesus needed to change the heart of Zacchaeus.

In this story, we see that many other people throughout Jericho were restored as well. Jesus had in mind a person and a city. He cared about Zacchaeus's heart *and* the people he had oppressed.

When Jesus rips evil from us, He rips evil from the world. When Jesus restores a heart, the world experiences the impact. God does not keep a scorecard. You are not ahead of the game simply because your sin is less obvious than someone else's transgressions.

There is no condemnation in Christ Jesus, or in the community that wears His name. The love of God is just as available to Fred Phelps as to those who rejoiced when he died. With God, it's all grace.

God's grace is unfair, and that is cause for celebration.

8

A Symphony of Grace

What Song Do We Overhear from Heaven?

Without music life would be a mistake.
— Friedrich Nietzsche

September 11, 2011, fell on a Sunday. If it hadn't, it would have been easy for churches to go about their usual Sunday-morning business like it was just another gathering.

But because it was the tenth anniversary of this great tragedy, churches all over America were caught in the awkward position of acknowledging the violence that caused the death of thousands of innocent people, but proclaiming the gospel of a Man who calls people to love their enemies.

So at the church where I (Jonathan) preach, we asked a man to share his testimony. His name is Ahmed and he moved from Iran to Abilene, Texas, about twenty years ago. He grew up in a strict Muslim home, and his move to Texas was his first experience of not living under Sharia law.

His first home in Abilene was just a block from our church, and at first he was confused why so many cars were parked outside his home on Sundays. Eventually Ahmed's curiosity got the better of him, and he wandered into the church building. Anyone who has grown up in America, and especially in a majority-Christian environment, might be unaware of how daunting an experience this is for someone from another religion.

Ahmed had no idea whether he was allowed to even enter a church. He was, after all, a Muslim. He expected to be thrown out, so he arrived late, sat in the back, and left before the service was over.

Then he came back the next week, and the next, and the next. Over the course of a few months, he started singing to Jesus. At first he didn't believe any of the words; he just thought the songs were beautiful. But eventually it dawned on him that something was happening inside him. To his great surprise, he had come to believe that Jesus was the Son of God.

But his spiritual transformation didn't start with a theological debate or a sermon or even a prayer. It started with a song.

THE PRODIGAL CAME HOME TO A PARTY

In chapter 7, we looked at the prodigal son story in Luke 15. One of the best parts of that story comes when Jesus describes the party scene. He uses a specific, very fascinating word. When the older brother heard music and dancing, the word Jesus uses for "music" in the Greek is *symphonias*. It's where we get the English word *symphony*.

People have gathered for a party as an overjoyed father celebrates the return of his younger son. A symphony of grace is playing. As the younger brother gets the restoration he doesn't deserve, his dutiful, stay-at-home, older brother gripes about God's not giving him what he feels he is owed.

The struggle on the part of the older brother reflects what was taking place in the hearts of first-century Jews who were deciding whether to follow Jesus. The news about eternal life was breathtaking, yet embracing it would mean becoming part of a new movement. They could accept a new identity that would launch them into a brand-new mission. Changing the world began with rethinking the old labels and changing allegiances.

No longer did it matter if you were Jew or Gentile, slave or free, male or female. In Christ you were given a new identity that redirected your passions, desires, and allegiances. It gave new direction, new passion, and new energy for things that matter.

It's interesting that the older brother—the one who saw himself as loyal and obedient—wanted nothing to do with a new identity. He was angry and resentful, and we see no indication in the story that he changed from being angry and resentful. Meanwhile, the younger brother, who had done everything wrong, was experiencing a new restoration. The parable ends with the father asking his older son to enter into the joy of celebration, and we lean in for the son's answer. We hear nothing.

The story of the prodigal fades to black with no proper finale. It is *The Sopranos* of the New Testament. That is, unless you read the Acts of the Apostles. Acts is the sequel, the *Empire Strikes Back* to the world we enter in the Gospel of Luke.

And in the book of Acts, we find the story of a flesh-and-blood older brother. Saul, a dutiful and zealous Pharisee, is the real counterpart to the fictional brother in Jesus's parable. Saul doesn't like Jesus, and he hates Christians.

Jesus had returned to His Father after inviting everyone to the feast that would restore them in all ways and reconcile them to God. But the Father noticed that many were not taking advantage of the invitation. One man in particular attracted Jesus's attention. In Acts 9, Saul is traveling to Damascus when Jesus stops him on the road. And everything changes.

I don't know why the Gospel of Luke is the only place in the New Testament where we read the story of the prodigal son. I don't know if Paul ever heard this story. But I am convinced that he knew it.

He was living it.

Saul could not be a more accurate portrayal of the older brother. His life gives us the ending of the story that Jesus left without a fitting conclusion. In Saul's version, the prideful older brother changed his mind and decided to come to the party. And he spent the rest of his life trying to get everyone else to join it.

POETRY, NOT SLAVERY

Jesus changed Saul's name to Paul, and Paul ended up writing much of what we now have as the New Testament. In a letter written to a group of churches, called Ephesians, Paul lays out a working understanding of God's grace. God's grace is a gift. It cannot be earned, so no one can boast.

Paul learned two things that have a bearing on his understanding of God's grace. First, God is not Pharaoh. Second, proud people don't know how to celebrate.

Paul went on to write: "For we are God's handiwork, created in Christ Jesus to do good works, which God prepared in advance for us to do" (Ephesians 2:10). The Greek word for "work" used here is *poeima*. It's where we get the English words *poem* and *poetry*.

God's work isn't slavery. The work that He made us for and is preparing us for in advance is *poetry*. Paul's use of this word points out a difference between the brothers in Jesus's story. The humbled younger brother who had returned home hoping he might work as a slave in his father's household was welcomed and celebrated. His father's welcoming response was abundant reason to do the work of his father. The younger brother was convinced of having received his father's blessing.

But the other brother, having never left home and feeling entitled to a better deal, had been working all along in the hope of receiving his father's blessing. You can do good things for the wrong reasons. And you can serve the wrong god—the god of duty, responsibility, appearances, status, or reputation. If you serve the wrong god, you will be disappointed when finally you are confronted by the incredible goodness of the real God. Like the older brother, you will resent the fact that God is so generous in His love and grace toward those who are the least deserving.

There is a difference between working for God and working with God. One is slavery; one is poetry. Do we slave for God, or can we be and write poetry with Him?

PAUL, THE PASSIONATE PASTOR

Paul was a pastor to rank-and-file Christians and to church leaders. He cared deeply about the people, their spiritual health, their struggles, and their witness to the world. This is why Paul used different approaches, and even a different tone of voice, depending on which congregation he was addressing in his letters.

When he wrote to Christians in Galatia, he came out swinging. The letter has no friendly preamble, no ice-breaker, no chitchat. Paul jumps right in, saying something along these lines: "I, Paul, sent by God. There is grace and peace. WHAT ARE YOU THINKING?" He comes across like a cop who gives speeding tickets for going three over. It's like a referee giving a flagrant foul to a player who simply shrugged his shoulders after colliding with another player.

Check this out:

Galatians 1:6–7—"I am astonished that you are so quickly deserting the one who called you to live in the grace of Christ and are turning to a different gospel—which is really no gospel at all. Evidently some people are throwing you into confusion and are trying to pervert the gospel of Christ."

3:1—"You foolish Galatians! Who has bewitched you?"

4:9–11—"But now that you know God—or rather are known by God—how is it that you are turning back to those weak and miserable forces? Do you wish to be enslaved by them all over again? You are observing special days and months and seasons and years! I fear for you, that somehow I have wasted my efforts on you."

5:2—"Mark my words! I, Paul, tell you that if you let yourselves be circumcised, Christ will be of no value to you at all."

5:7—"You were running a good race. Who cut in on you to keep you from obeying the truth?"

5:11–12—"Brothers and sisters, if I am still preaching circumcision, why am I still being persecuted? In that case the offense of the cross has been abolished. As for those agitators, I wish they would go the whole way and emasculate themselves!"

At that point, if children were still in the room, their moms and dads were placing hands over the kids' ears. But a youngster in the back of the room was heard asking, "Mommy, what does *emasculate* mean?"

Does Paul sound harsh? Yes. Does he also sound like a man who is deeply invested in the formation of hearts? Absolutely. He comes on strong because the problem is so damaging. It is this: we can make a mess out of God's gift of life.

We can lose our focus and our moral compass. We can make a mess of love. Love doesn't fight to preserve what worked in the past. Instead, love has legs and arms and movement. Love is rooted in hope that the future will be embraced as offering opportunities for God's continued faithfulness!

The Jesus-followers in Galatia had gotten sidetracked. As individuals they were immoral, promiscuous, and materialistic. As a faith community, they were legalistic and shallow.

Yet Paul knew the song of Scripture. He was familiar with the tune, rhythm, cadence, and dance of God. He knew that a favorite type of song heard in Scripture is a restoration song. That is likely why he used an image of music to call Christians deeper into life with God.

Galatians 6:1: "If someone is caught in a sin, you who live by the Spirit should restore that person gently." The Greek word for *restore* is a musical term. Paul's image for what the church needed was *restoration set to music.*

Restoration and hope capture the story of God from Genesis to Revelation. Maybe you've noticed how the first two chapters of Genesis function poetically. In the Hebrew, there's a rhythm to the language. There is melody and a beat. It's a dance.

The rhythm can be followed if you look for this: God creates, then God says, "It is good."

> God separated the waters.
> And it is good.
> God created plants and vegetation.
> And it is good.
> God created wild animals.
> And it is good.
> God created a man.
> And it is good.
> God created the woman.
>   And it is *very* good.

Genesis 1 is a work of art, because the world God created for us is a work of art, and God is a very good Artist. God speaks, creation happens, God cares.

God creates because God is extravagant. Then He applauds creation, because it is beautiful, the work of God's hands.

Then creation made a mess of God's love.

If it is true that Genesis 1 and 2 sing a song of unity, harmony, rhythm, balance, and perfection, we must ask, Who doesn't want to sing that song? Every genre of music points to the song of Genesis 1 and 2, even if listeners aren't aware of it. From hip-hop's raw depictions of life to country music's songs about dogs being left behind with the ex-wife, they are songs that long for something better. They crave hope.

Restoration songs are the songs heaven still sings. They are the songs that still invade our world.

If earth is heaven's womb, what song do we overhear from heaven?

MISSING GOD'S TUNE

Jonathan and I grew up in a Christian tradition that is known for singing. It's funny, because even though four-part harmony has been in our history for a long time, neither Jonathan nor I have any clue what part we sing. The ability to carry a tune skipped over us.

It showed one Sunday morning when I (Josh) agreed to fill in for a friend who pastored a church outside Abilene, Texas. Kayci and I drove in our 1995 Ford Ranger to a little church outside town. My friend had told me I'd be preaching to about fifteen people, but if one family was gone, we could be down to seven people.

I went prepared to preach and to teach a combined Sunday school class. When we arrived, I discovered I also had the opening and closing prayer, the prayers for the bread, cup, and offering, and I was also the only one in position to pass the tray. There were other adults present, but they weren't as mobile.

Worst of all, I had to lead singing. I've never been shy speaking and praying in front of an audience, but the thought of leading singing terrifies me. I stood up in front of the church and froze. I began to think about what I'd seen others do. In our faith heritage, there is a cadence when the song leader calls out songs. It goes something like this, "Please turn to number 482 ... 4 ... 8 ... 2." It's the full number followed by each individual number. So that's what I did.

People turned to the correct page in the songbook. Then I froze again because I didn't know how to start a song. I knew that song leaders move their hand in a motion to guide the song. I wasn't sure what to do with my hand, but I began moving it. The song started, and the congregation began to sing.

That's when I saw my wife lift one of her hands in the air, then she placed her other hand on top of it, and she quickly dropped both hands, as if to say, "Put your hand down. You aren't doing it right, and it is embarrassing me."

Kayci sat in the middle of the group of fifteen people. I have the most encouraging wife in the world. I never doubt that she is my biggest fan. But that day she sat through the song service with the songbook in front of her face while her shoulders bounced because she was laughing so hard.

On the way home we laughed about the time I wrote her a song and performed it for her. We had been dating for a few months, and I thought it would be cool to write her a song to celebrate and describe our relationship. It consisted of four verses, a chorus, and a bridge. It was called "You Are My Princess." If you're laughing now, wait until you hear the rest.

I got down on a knee and began singing the song to her. I could tell she was moved by the content. It was well thought out. Yet, after the second verse she leaned down and said, "It's beautiful. But do you think you can just speak the last two verses and not sing them?"

My brother is an anointed worship leader. My dad was a drummer with Ronnie Dunn (from Brooks and Dunn) in college, before Ronnie relocated to Nashville. My sister's voice was one of the purest I've ever heard. But me? I'm a tune glitch waiting to happen.

Have you known those people? They can't read music and can't carry a note. You probably know more people who are out of tune with the rhythm of God. Rhythm is important. I know this because Paul reminded the Christians in Galatia of rhythm.

> Brothers and sisters, if someone is caught in a sin, you who live by the Spirit should restore that person gently. But watch yourselves, or you also may be tempted. Carry each other's burdens, and in this way you will fulfill the law of Christ. If anyone thinks they are something when they are not, they deceive themselves. Each one should test their own actions. Then they can take pride in themselves alone, without comparing themselves to someone else, for each one should carry their own load. (Galatians 6:1–5)

If you decide to confront people over their sin, and as you do so you are comparing your own moral behavior to their failings, you are in spiritual danger. When you compare your strengths against another person's weaknesses, you become the older brother in Luke 15.

Look at the younger brother in Jesus's parable. He had broken every commandment except possibly the prohibition against adultery. And that was only because, to our knowledge, he had never married. The older brother looked down on his brother, returning as a broken, dissipated man. The older brother might rightly have felt that he had resisted sleeping around, gambling, drunkenness, and other excesses. He did have one addiction, pride, but most likely he was not aware of it.

The older brother would have agreed that a welcome-home party was in order, but only after the younger brother had confessed in front of everyone, giving a heartfelt apology. And then, just to make sure, perhaps the offender should be put on probationary status for a year or so. Just to prove himself.

That is how a lot of people miss the life God has invited us into through Jesus.

THE RESTORATIVE WORK OF GOD'S SPIRIT

The Holy Spirit restores us in a spirit of gentleness. God's Spirit invades and indwells, then gives responsibility. We are responsible to restore others in a spirit of gentleness.

Three Greek words are translated in English-language New Testaments as "restore." The one used in Galatians 6:1 is *katartizo*. It means "to mend" or "be ye attuning" or "to be tuned." Mark Buchanan, in his book *Your Church Is Too Safe,* shows how *katartizo* paints a picture of an instrument capable of producing beautiful, resonant, evocative music, but badly out of tune.

Buchanan wrote: "It needs a gentle, masterful touch, a tightening here, a loosening there, a lowering of the strings or a straightening of the neck, a slow, painstaking removal of grime and a lavish, penetrating kneading-in of oil, to restore it to its true potential."[1]

Before a band takes the stage, the guitarist tunes her instrument. She doesn't wear a tool belt so that when her guitar doesn't sound right, she can pull out a hammer and hit it. Roughing up an instrument will only make it worse. The only way to get it back in tune is to use a gentle touch.

Paul told the Christians in Galatia to gently care for those who were not living in tune with the ways of God. They were to step into the mess in order to offer love, grace, and healing. To step into a mess, or to step into the life of someone who has made a mess, doesn't mean you are endorsing the mess. It simply means you're moving with God. We don't step in with hammers, saws, and machetes. We gently restore someone with time, love, and abiding presence.

Restored people restore people.

CANTUS FIRMUS

In the days of Gregorian chant, the *cantus firmus* was the bass line, the center. All the other parts could be added on. These parts could adapt and shift as long as the *cantus firmus,* the solid song, this enduring melody, remained stable.

Christians talk about a Christian worldview or a Christian philosophy or Christian narrative, and all those things are decent enough ways of talking about the Jesus story. But I have fallen in love with the *cantus firmus,* the song of God, echoing through the ages. God's song is heard the world over by people who are sinners and saints, prostitutes and prodigals.

The gospel of Jesus is that the Father never stops looking. He loves to restore people who finally have come to their senses enough to be able to hear the restoration song. God has been singing it since life went wrong in the garden. God always is putting on a symphony of grace for those who come home.

It is said that when Beethoven breathed his last breath, he said, "I shall hear in Heaven."

It. Is. Good.

9

Jesus Throws the Best Parties

The Church Is at Its Best When
It Gives Up Home-Field Advantage

> The church used to give the best parties.
> Festivals were noisy, multisensory, sensual
> events with party planners who were the
> leading artists of their day. . . . Now it seems
> many Christians are allergic to parties, if not
> outright opposed to them.
>
> — Leonard Sweet

> A dead thing can go with the stream, but
> only a living thing can go against it.
>
> — G. K. Chesterton

Before I (Josh) moved to Memphis, I was pastor of a church in Houston. For many years, we would throw an annual party with barbecue hot off the grill, cold watermelons, and plenty of sodas. We'd hand out fliers in advance, inviting everyone in the neighborhood to join us. On the day of the big party, church people would gather, the meat would be grilling, watermelon and drinks would be on ice. We would wait in anticipation for our neighbors to arrive.

Except they wouldn't come.

Fliers and invitations weren't working, so we decided to take a lesson from Jesus. When He fellowshipped with people, it wasn't on the grounds of a synagogue. He wasn't anti-Temple, anti-synagogue, or anti–religious space, but Jesus did model a way of taking the good news of God into every possible space. He hosted meals in homes, healed people in alleys, taught people and cared for them in fields, spent time in places where sick people huddled together like refugees. More than inviting people onto religious space so they could be tended to, Jesus worked His way into the grind of everyday life.

Clearly, Jesus knew what He was doing.

So we approached an apartment complex that sits across the street from the church facility, asking the building management if we could host a cookout on the complex's courtyard. The more we looked at Jesus, the more we were convinced that the church often is at its best when it gives up home-field advantage. If we were serious about connecting with our neighbors, we needed to throw a party where the neighbors live. We knew we couldn't do church parties on church space any longer.

I expected the apartment manager would have some questions about our agenda. Did we plan to hand out tracts? Were we going to give an altar call? Would we only give burgers to people who agreed to visit our church?

We were surprised when she got excited about the idea. However, she had one suggestion. She wanted us to come during the week, to avoid the Saturday-evening-to-Sunday-evening period, which at this apartment complex coincided with heavy drinking. But we chose to stick with Sunday afternoon. The church people could decide what to do if they were offered a cold Bud or a shot of Jack in good fellowship.

We did have two rules:

Rule #1: This isn't a church event. If you plan to attend the barbecue and associate only with church folks, we would rather you go to a nearby restaurant.

Rule #2: If you bring a lawn chair for yourself, you need to bring a lawn chair for a neighbor.

At that time, the congregation was made up primarily of older white people. But settled and self-satisfied they weren't. They were some of the most energetic people I have ever known. They were pursuing God and living adventurously for Jesus.

The apartment complex, in contrast, was home to young minorities. On the day of the barbecue, as our people crossed the street carrying food and lawn chairs, I guarantee our neighbors had never seen so many gray-haired white people advancing toward them. It was like *Field of Dreams,* but without the cornfield. We just kept coming.

As we gathered around the grill, you could see people peeking through window blinds. Then we noticed some doors were opening. Then people began to make their way into the courtyard. For two hours, we ate burgers and hotdogs, drank sodas, and fellowshipped. I watched church members who are known to be introverts engage in spirited conversations with new friends. I witnessed people who could only speak English converse with new friends who could only speak Spanish. It felt like Acts 2 all over again.

Some may call what we did a barbecue. Some may call it simply fellowshipping with neighbors. I think the Bible calls it a *party.* That day, the neighborhood began to change.

From then on, our parties took place off campus. We took the spirit of celebration into the world, and it worked. Sometimes you don't know you're at a Kingdom party until you are *part of* a Kingdom party.

THE PROPHET OF POTLUCKS

Jesus always seems to be going to or coming from a party, and He gets in trouble with religious leaders because of it. They don't approve of His party-going habits or the people He likes to party with.

For Jesus, sitting around a table with friends and strangers was a place where the world was set right. Good food and drink were important, but along with that, relationships were being formed and healing and restoration took place. It wasn't that Jewish leaders missed the point of what Jesus was doing, it was actually the opposite. They knew the power of a table; their problem was that Jesus was so indiscriminate when He partied.

We see this in the Gospel of Luke. Chapter 14 opens with Jesus, a meal, a Pharisee's house, more Pharisees, and a Sabbath day. That makes for a potent combination. It would be like Donald Trump, Hillary Clinton, Oprah, Justin Bieber, and Vladimir Putin getting together over breakfast. Sparks are bound to fly. Whenever Jesus and Pharisees were around one another, tension was in the air. Pretty much all it took was a Sabbath. Jesus was sure to say or do something that would set things off.

A man suffering from dropsy came to Jesus. Dropsy is the building up of bodily fluids under the skin. It can be quite painful. The man appeared just as Jesus was about to eat a meal in the home of a Pharisee.

Jesus and the Pharisees both had a love for Scripture, but Jesus tended to ask questions that went beyond "What do the Scriptures say?" Jesus would ask, "What is the value of a human being?"

At the Pharisee's house, no one said anything when Jesus healed the man with dropsy. There was no celebration, no words of congratulation, nothing.

But those present did pay attention to the seating chart. Table seating was about honor. The closer you were seated to the head of the table, the more important you were. The men at this dinner cared too much about status, so Jesus told them a story about jockeying for seats of honor. He ended with this:

> When you give a luncheon or dinner, do not invite your friends,
> your brothers or sisters, your relatives, or your rich neighbors; if
> you do, they may invite you back and so you will be repaid. But
> when you give a banquet, invite the poor, the crippled, the lame,
> the blind, and you will be blessed. Although they cannot repay
> you, you will be repaid at the resurrection of the righteous. (Luke
> 14:12–14)

Jesus was referring to a party. It was a party that included people you don't know, and what's more, they would be people you have very little in common with. The Pharisees did not come from the same neighborhood as the poor, the lame, and the blind. Is anyone, anywhere throwing parties like this?

Jesus loved telling stories about parties. He continued this story by adding another scene. Certain people were invited to a party, but they refused to come. So new invitations were sent out.

Here is a breakdown of the action:

- A man with dropsy showed up at a home where Jesus was
  having dinner. The man, due to his illness, was swollen.
  (Another way of saying that is to say that he was puffed
  up.)
- It was the Sabbath, yet Jesus healed the man. The Pharisees
  at the dinner were silent. They could not believe Jesus
  would heal someone on the Sabbath.
- Jesus told His host and the dinner guests a story about
  people who want the best seats in the house.

- Jesus was painting a picture in words, helping His listeners imagine how the Kingdom of heaven creates new parties that include all people.
- Jesus sketched out what that looks like in real life. Heaven is a lot like life on earth that reaches all people.

The Pharisees had been silent when Jesus healed the man and in their view had violated the Sabbath. But they stayed true to form when they sought status by means of the seating arrangement at the table. The man with dropsy was healed. Who was left at the dinner who was *really* puffed up? One of the symptoms of dropsy is that you are always thirsty. Even though water is what's killing you, you can't get enough. These two stories go together because both parties wanted something that was killing them, but only one of them knew it was a disease.

The Pharisees were worried about who got to sit nearest the head of the table. But when Jesus heals, restores, and redeems people, it's time to bring out decorations and party hats. No one gets pushed to the margins; all are invited.

A PARTY THAT DOESN'T NEED BOUNCERS

Most of us have seen Jesus-celebrations done right, and we have seen them done wrong. When I (Josh) was a senior in high school, I was part of a group of Christians that got excited about sharing Jesus with the world. Back then, in Dallas, the place to dive into deep conversations was CiCi's Pizza. It was the busiest CiCi's in the country.

The owner has led more people to Jesus than anyone else I know. He would share Jesus with the managers he would hire, employees, customers who came to him with questions, even people he encountered on the beach when he was on vacation.

One man the CiCi's owner had led to Christ had a sister who was an exotic dancer, yet she was looking for a better way to live. One day she gave her life over to Jesus and was baptized. As she came out of the water, she was met by a church elder. Standing there next to her, and in front of other people, the elder said: "It's time for you to begin dressing more appropriately." She was humiliated, and she didn't come back.

This woman had the courage to follow Jesus in baptism. It took faith and commitment to do what she did. She loved Jesus, and she deserved a party, not a put-down. She finally had returned home and should have been given a robe, a ring, and a loud welcome with music and dancing. At least that is the kind of party that took place in the stories Jesus told. But instead, she was met with a frowning elder who was determined to "set her straight."

We have talked already about the prodigal son story in Luke 15. But other stories precede the one about a son who went wild. When a sheep went missing, the shepherd left the other ninety-nine sheep in the herd to search for the one that was lost. When a woman discovered she had lost a coin, she searched her home until she found it.

Before Jesus told stories about the lost being sought out, a displeased religious leader had accused him with these words: "This man welcomes sinners and eats with them" (Luke 15:2). In response to that, Jesus unleashed story after story.

To the Pharisees, a party was a celebration thrown for the privileged. But Jesus came to introduce people to the type of celebrations that are held in heaven. In the stories about sheep and a coin, when the lost item was found, a party was thrown.

Then came the lengthy story of the prodigal son. The younger son left home with his inheritance, wasted it, and finally "came to his senses" (Luke 15:17). When he returned home, he saw that his father was ready to greet him. The father saw his son coming, and he ran to meet him. It's the only place in the Bible where God is portrayed as being in a hurry. It makes you wonder if the only thing that can make God move quickly is a party that is waiting to happen.

The father in the story had every right to give his younger son a lecture. But instead, he threw a big party. It was such a great party that Jesus says you could hear "music and dancing." It's one thing to hear music, but when you can hear *dancing,* you know it's a true shindig.

We have been pastors for a combined twenty-five years. In that time we have heard of churches that refuse to throw baby showers for unmarried women. Maybe it's because these Christians don't want it to look as if they condone sex outside marriage. Perhaps the churches feel the new mother first needs to face some form of punishment. It just seems that Jesus would have done something different.

The parties Jesus threw didn't have the effect of approving excess or sin. His parties made people want to *flee* sin and evil. People left His parties wanting to live better lives, to be different people. And this is where the local church needs to lean into Jesus's way of doing things. If it is true that God is still just as creative as He was in the first two chapters of Genesis, then God can help us get creative with how we throw parties.

A few years ago, I (Josh) preached a sermon from Luke 15, highlighting how each of the three stories told in that chapter ends with a party. Throughout the following week, God began to move in the heart of a young man who had gone wild with drugs, promiscuity, and other forms of evil. When he surrendered his life to Jesus, he was baptized. That's when the church came to me and said, "We need a cake. We need cookies. You preached about Jesus throwing parties, so let's do it!" Jesus mentioned three things that had been lost and then were found. This young man was found by God, and he gladly responded to his Father. We needed to throw a party.

I went out and bought a cake and we had a party. According to Jesus,

"We had to celebrate and be glad, because this brother of yours was dead and is alive again; he was lost and is found" (Luke 15:32).

WHAT JESUS HOLDS BACK

There are those who party in ways that are immoral and self-gratifying. Others avoid celebrations, even genuine Jesus-celebrations, seeking to uphold their religiosity. Both types of people need a better understanding of Jesus's mission.

We both grew up going to church camp during the summers. At camp, a lot of kids got baptized, but we were not allowed to celebrate. We were told that baptism was about reverence and awe. We were told not to clap or to shout for joy. But Jesus said when the lost are found, parties are in order. I prefer to believe Jesus in this matter.

I never want to be blinded to the truth that life is a gift and God is the Life of the party. In his book *Orthodoxy*, G. K. Chesterton wrote that we tacitly, and wrongly, assume that since we have discovered how some things in the natural world work, that must mean God is no longer intimately involved in holding all things together. Just because we are accustomed to the sun rising each day doesn't mean that the solar system, the Milky Way, or other galaxies are closed. Perhaps God takes such great joy in creating things that He never stopped creating. Chesterton offered this fresh understanding:

> It is possible that God says every morning, "Do it again" to the sun; and every evening, "Do it again" to the moon. It may not be automatic necessity that makes all daisies alike; it may be that God makes every daisy separately, but has never got tired of making them. It may be that He has the eternal appetite of infancy; for we have sinned and grown old, and our Father is

younger than we. The repetition in Nature may not be a mere recurrence; it may be a theatrical *encore*.[1]

Chesterton ended the book by writing about the difference between Jesus and other great people of history. Other great leaders tower over the common people to make themselves seem important. When Jesus walked into a room, no one was diminished. Rather, He seemed almost casual in His interactions.

Further, Jesus showed strength through compassion. He wept openly about things as common as seeing the city skyline. But Chesterton pointed out there was one thing that Jesus had to hold back. The one thing He was rather shy about was His great joy.

Jesus loved to party, and He violated religious and social norms when He chose the crowd He would party with. At times, the party guests included religious leaders and experts in the law. But more typically, party goers were people commonly referred to as "sinners." Jesus saw reasons to celebrate in ways that we need to be aware of today. And once we are aware, we need to party like Jesus did.

The Bible's picture of salvation often looks like an invitation to a feast in heaven. If you know what is going on in heaven, you have a picture of what things should look like on earth. We can help bring heaven to earth, and that's reason for celebration.

We believe the day is coming when death will die.

We believe the clock is ticking on injustice.

We believe God soon will break to pieces the plans of the Enemy.

We believe that a day is on its way when Satan is not going to be able to win anything.

And so we can start celebrating now because we believe Jesus is the Life of the party on earth as He is in heaven.

10

A Party Waiting to Happen

Jesus Insists on Including the Most Unlikely People

Last night I went to a party. Everyone
admired my wit and sophistication. All
agreed that I was most entertaining. And I
returned to my apartment, closed the door,
held a gun in my hands and thought about
blowing out my brains.

— Sören Kierkegaard

The call came a little before ten o'clock on a dull Monday morning in
April. The caller said her name was Susan. She called the church
where I (Jonathan) work because when she was a girl, the bus ministry
had picked her up a few times for Sunday school. She had trouble getting
all this out due to her agitated state of mind. But she didn't know where
else to turn.

The day Susan called, her brother Eddie was dying. He had learned
four months earlier that he had stomach cancer. All attempts to stop its
spread had failed, and Susan knew that Eddie wasn't saved. Eddie knew it

too. Susan asked if I could come and help save her brother's soul. Since he was already in hospice care, Susan wanted me to come as soon as possible.

DEATH BEDS AND THIN SPACES

Later that day, my intern, Jake, and I drove out to the rural home where Eddie was spending his final days on earth. We were ushered into the living room, where we met Eddie's family. His sons, daughter, and sister were grateful we had come. They tried to express how important it was to know that Eddie would be going to heaven.

Then we met Lisa. It turned out that Eddie had more people than just children and siblings in his life. He had a wife, and she was not aware that pastors had been invited to visit Eddie.

Death draws out whatever dysfunctions a family has, and this family had its share. Lisa was surprised that two strangers would come into her home during this very intimate time of saying good-bye. She asked a long series of questions to find out who we were and who had invited us.

At one point, Susan turned to Eddie's son and asked in a whisper: "Will you say you called them? I think it'll go better if she thinks this was your idea." (Susan, of course, had made the call to the church.) We found out the son didn't want the wrath of his stepmother turned on him. But Susan was not to be deterred. She asked me to say that the son had made the call.

I suggested the two sons go to their dad to see what he'd like to do. Unfortunately, I hadn't thought this through completely. The sons were gone for about thirty minutes, leaving us in a room with Eddie's wife—the one person present who, without question, did not want us to be there.

There are days that I wonder why I didn't become a plumber.

The family had different perspectives on Eddie's eternal soul. His wife, Lisa, was certain he was already saved. She saw him as a saint. However, the other people in the room were certain that Eddie was a bona fide sinner. If heaven worked on a majority-vote system, Eddie was doomed.

I don't want to diminish this moment. They were terrified for their dad and brother. Grown men were crying and begging us to help. But Lisa wouldn't budge.

She said Eddie had been going to church and that she had a pastor who would come out. She indicated that her pastor was better qualified to save Eddie's soul. While she said this, the rest of the family kept whispering in my ear, "Don't believe her. They haven't been going to church, and she's not calling anyone else."

When people are dying or have passed on, the family members give a minister the most reverent description of their lives. Buried underneath this peculiar phenomenon, I think, is a certain idea about God. We think that if we can get the minister to believe that a person is virtuous, then both God and the pastor will be fooled. Behind this odd idea is the suspicion that God isn't just dumb, but bad.

People often fear that God is out to get them and that nothing would make Him happier than to send them and their loved one to hell. They feel like if they can mislead God's representative (the minister), then maybe they'll all have a chance at getting the go-ahead to enter heaven.

I decided to sidestep the "Should we save Eddie?" controversy. Instead, I suggested we talk about how they might be able to say good-bye to their brother and father, whom they all loved very much.

I asked them to tell me about Eddie. He had been a great dad; he had worked hard to provide for his family; and he always kept his word. He had been abused as a child but had worked hard to break that cycle before it affected how he related to his own children. He hadn't had a particularly deep spiritual life, but his mother had passed away a few years earlier and she had begged him on her deathbed to please get right with God.

Now that Eddie was on his deathbed, the time left to grant her request was winding down. That's why they had called the only church they knew to come out and help.

In the middle of the chaos, I told them the story about the thief on the cross. Jesus was killed between two criminals, people who deserved the kind of death they were receiving. I told them how one of the criminals did the hardest thing for people like that to do. He asked Jesus for help. He had faith that a man who was hanging on a cross, dying at the same time and in the same way he was, could do something for him in the Age to Come. Jesus said to this man, "Today you will be with me in paradise" (Luke 23:43).

I don't know much about that thief, but he wasn't always a thief. At one point he was someone's little boy. He had dreams of being someone else, someone better. But like all of us, the choices we make tend to snowball until often we find ourselves becoming people we hardly recognize. When this man came to his senses, it appears that it was too late to do anything about it. Almost.

Jesus took notice of the man's request. In Jesus's final breaths, breaths that cost Him because of the extreme pressure on His lungs, Jesus spoke to the criminal. He said something that would have sounded like, "Today I will make the sad things of your life come untrue."

This story shouldn't surprise anyone who has paid attention to Jesus's preaching (and parties) up to this point. He was simply practicing what He had preached during three years of public ministry. I told Eddie's family there is a reason this story is recorded only by Luke, the same gospel writer who gave us the story of the prodigal son.

The story of Jesus and the criminal talking while the two of them were hanging on separate crosses shows us what the wayward-son story looks like when it's not a parable. In this account, the criminal is the wayward son in real life, coming to his senses and coming home to the only One who could save him.

Eddie's family was not familiar with the prodigal son story. So I mentioned that Jesus had told a story to the religious people of His day. A father was hoping his son would come home. In fact, he was confident that someday the irresponsible son would appear back where he belonged. The father kept a lookout, hoping every day that he would spot his son in the distance. One day the father saw his son coming, and he ran to hug the son and welcome him back. The father threw a party to celebrate his son's return. The one who had been lost was now home.

This is who God really is. He wants us to come home so He can welcome us in. There is no need to try to trick Him or pretend to be something we're not. All we have to do is turn toward Him. He loves to come running to welcome us with love, a hug, and a party.

Lisa decided to let us go speak with Eddie.

When Jake and I walked into the room to meet Eddie, it was obvious that he was not long for this world. There is a tangible difference in rooms like this, as if a wave of holy air washes over you. Celtic Christians call moments such as this "thin spaces," where heaven and earth seem to overlap. Eddie had at one time weighed two hundred fifty pounds, and most of it was muscle. Now he weighed less than one hundred pounds. He was in great pain, and every breath was labored.

The family asked us to pray for Eddie to have peace as he went to meet God. We prayed, and we spoke with Eddie. "Eddie, I know you are worried about coming face-to-face with God. But I want you to know that when you see God, you are going to enjoy Him. Because He will enjoy seeing you. When you see God, contrary to what you've been thinking, God will be smiling."

For a very brief moment so was Eddie.

Each of us has a canon within a canon, a kind of lens that we read the Bible through. Some preachers read Scripture and emphasize the need for holiness. Others may emphasize social action and the need to work for God's justice in the world. All of these are important biblical themes.

When I left Eddie's house, I was determined that no one who heard my preaching for any length of time would continue to be unaware of the story of the prodigal son. It is the gospel within the gospel. For some reason, when Jesus wanted to explain His ministry, He told this story. If you are going to understand God, this kind of party is central.

Jesus is the Father who runs to us, even when we are still far from Him. He is always looking for us, and He sees us from a distance. He sees that we are approaching, even if we're doing so with doubts or shame—even if we fear that He will turn away from us. He sees us from afar, and He comes running toward us. He closes the gap between Himself and every person who approaches. He takes the initiative; He can't help it. In His great joy, He runs to us.

FROM HOLY NIGHTS AND HUMAN RIGHTS

My (Jonathan) favorite hymn is "O Holy Night."[1] It's easily one of the most profound, powerful songs ever sung. "Fall on your knees." This was not written as a request, but as a mandate. In the light of the gospel and the power of God's love and grace, we have no choice but to kneel in worship.

Heaven has entered earth in the form of a Baby, and now "the soul feels its worth." What a great line! The chains are released because the slave is our brother, because the soul feels its worth.

I think I understand why we keep this hymn in the "Christmas song" category. It conveys such power and insists on such a humble response that we can only handle it a couple of times a year. And from a historical standpoint, it's incredibly accurate.

When most of us think of human rights—when we think of equality and opportunity, justice and mercy—the biblical foundation for these things is entirely influenced by the Jesus story. Heaven has intersected earth and changed everything. The soul has felt its worth.

I often picture the scene of Jesus's entrance into the world. It was celebrated by shepherds, angels, Mary and Joseph, and the heavens. Within a few months even magicians from the East showed up with valuable gifts. By His presence on earth, Jesus was bringing God's party to us. And in His ministry and teaching, He was running toward all the prodigals *and* all the older brothers. The prodigals are getting to the end of their rope and have begun to suspect there is more to life than the pursuit of pleasure and selfish goals. And the older brothers have thought they were somehow above it all. But now, in Jesus's presence, they realize they were wrong.

All of us who have worked up excuses to try to explain why we left home; all of us who have been buried in shame due to past sin; all of us who stayed away from the party and tried to feel good about our self-righteousness . . . Jesus is God's Way of approaching us no matter what we have done, no matter how we feel about our lives, no matter our questions, doubts, or excuses.

Jesus is God's Way of letting the soul feel its worth. At its heart, the gospel is about a God who *chooses to be among us.*

God chooses to be among the people who ordinarily are overlooked. He pays special attention to shepherds and teenagers and fishermen and single moms and small children. Jesus shows special care to lepers, blind persons, those with physical disabilities, crooks, liars, hookers, and worse. That's who God has decided to be with.

THE WORTH OF A SOUL

René Girard was a French philosopher who taught at Stanford University. He was a brilliant anthropologist who was fascinated with one question:

Why, in modern times, does the "marginalized" person have moral authority?

This reality confused Girard because, outside of the movement of Jesus, there was nothing comparable to it in ancient culture or literature. The ancient world celebrated the strong and heroic, not the vulnerable and weak. Girard found this fascinating in light of greater attention being paid in the modern world to liberation movements and efforts to protect the rights of minorities and to combat human trafficking. What was motivating all these efforts to come to the aid of marginalized and powerless people?

Girard traced this social phenomenon back to the life of Jesus. He discovered that with His birth and death, Jesus introduced a new plot to human history. The victim mattered. The people who were oppressed mattered. And to the confusion of his peers at Stanford University, Girard, a man respected for being a great thinker and widely known as a secular humanist, started following Jesus.[2]

Our world thinks the most important thing you can do is take the right position on the right issues. Jesus reminds us that the most important thing is to be standing in the right place. Girard's great insight was that Jesus changed the world by standing in solidarity with all the "wrong" people.

Jesus created a new ethic, which His followers adopted and lived out. God in human flesh celebrated life among the least of these, until the outcasts and overlooked people on the margins of society started to realize that they mattered too. Gradually it took hold, so that a growing number of cultures adopted an ethic that insisted that everyone mattered. It sounds like such common sense to today's Western mind. After all, we assume that these truths are self-evident. But in Jesus's day, this was a breathtaking, groundbreaking insight that no one had ever considered before.

Who would have thought that asking a Samaritan divorcée for water, having a party with a corrupt tax collector, or touching lepers would have such far-reaching implications? Who would have thought that a Judean peasant who never wrote a word that was preserved, and who never travelled farther than forty miles from the village where He was born, would so radically alter the world? But centuries later, Jesus's life slowly deconstructed an economy in the West, in a world that was unknown to the ancient Near East. His life, example, and justice ethic overturned a system built on slave labor and slave trading. And He did it with parties. By choosing to socialize with those who were despised by the "acceptable" people, Jesus opened people's eyes to the entrenched lie that some lives matter more than others.

God in human flesh partied with *all the wrong people.*

Imagine There's No Heaven?

In his great book *Unapologetic,* the English author Francis Spufford objected to a notorious atheist slogan seen around London: "There's probably no God. Now stop worrying and enjoy your life."[3]

The most outrageous word in this advertisement, Spufford wrote, isn't the word *probably.* (In the words of comedian Louis C. K.: "I don't know if there's a God, but that's all I can say, honestly . . . Some people think that they know that there *isn't* . . . "Yeah . . . No, there's no God!" "How do you *know*?. . . . Did you look *everywhere*?")[4]

Spufford says the most outrageous word in the advertisement is *enjoy.* The slogan assumes that the default state of the universe is luxury and ease, and that the real problem is caused by religious worrywarts making everyone anxious with their Chicken-Little-the-sky-is-falling rhetoric. Spufford also points out that this is a theory that has been around for quite some time.

Readers of a certain age might remember a music video featuring

John Lennon and Yoko Ono for the song "Imagine." They made the video in a pristine white house, and Yoko is dressed in white. She goes around opening windows as Lennon plays a white piano crooning about a world without heaven. In such a world, the song suggests, all people would live in peace.[5]

Without heaven, John and Yoko pictured a world where everyone lays down their weapons, where we stop hoarding, and where we abolish hunger and poverty. Imagine a world without religion, without heaven or hell, and maybe life will become more like an open, pristine, white room where peace abounds.

Imagine indeed.

Spufford critiqued Lennon's rejection of religion:

Imagine all the people living life in—hello? Excuse me? Take religion out of the picture, and suddenly everyone spontaneously starts living life in *peace*? I don't know about you, but in my experience peace is not the default state of human beings. . . . Peace is not the norm; peace is rare. . . . I'm not at peace all that often, and I doubt you are either. I'm absolutely bloody certain that John Lennon wasn't. The mouthy Scouse . . . who allegedly kicked his best friend in the head in Hamburg, didn't just go away. . . . What seems to be at work in "Imagine" is the idea— always beloved by those who are frightened of themselves—that we're good underneath, good by nature, and only do bad things because we've been forced out of shape by some external force.[6]

John Lennon had a great imagination. But he sorely misdiagnosed the problem, not to mention the solution.

Throughout the centuries, the people who thought the most about a future guided by God's desires are the same people who have done the most to serve human needs. Lennon's lyrics sounded novel, but they were closer to the Old Testament prophets' imagination for a day when swords would be beaten into plowshares and justice would roll like a river. Lennon pictured a world without greed and need, and with conflict replaced by a single brotherhood of humanity. He pictured, in short, the biblical idea of heaven, then he subverted his own poetry by imagining there isn't one.

The wealthy and privileged might have the luxury of insulating themselves from the suffering of the world, and they might accept their isolation as a form of peace. But the rest of us are regularly enmeshed in the pain and loss of those around us. I have attended too many funerals and visited too many cancer wards, jail cells, courtrooms, and halfway houses to believe that the default state of the human condition is one to easily "enjoy."

Eventually, every one of us—privileged or not, wealthy or not—will have to face the ways we have contributed to the sorrow of the world. Even those who pursue the party life as a way to shield themselves from the reality everyone else is experiencing can't keep it up forever.

But there are much better parties, celebrations that put us in touch with the work and the ways of God, and Jesus knows how to throw such parties. Before Jesus tells the story of the prodigal son, there's a pivotal verse where Luke tells us that Jesus "resolutely set out for Jerusalem" (9:51). The sentence frames the rest of Luke's Gospel. It means that Jesus was heading somewhere intentionally. He was going to die.

THE LIFE OF THE PARTY

Luke described dozens of parties that Jesus attended or hosted, and almost every one took place *after* that verse. For Jesus, death would not be the final word to be spoken. In fact, facing death—not avoiding it—was the best way to really live. And it still is.

Jesus didn't throw parties to distract His thinking from His impending death; He partied as He squarely faced death. All along the way to His own death, Jesus gathered around Him the wrong people and kept saying the most annoying things about the ways we have carved up the world to keep one another at arm's length.

And then He died, and life for those who had followed Him went back to normal.

Until . . .

The Life of the party broke through death.

We tend to think of the cross of Jesus as the way God dealt with our sins. But if death entered the world as sin, then the resurrection *is the forgiveness of sins.*

Jesus's resurrection is God's way of saying there is nothing that you have done or can do in the future that could exclude you from a party that Jesus is throwing for eternity. It is God's way of saying, *"The parties that Jesus has been throwing and attending are in tune with who I am."* The resurrection of Jesus was more than just God bringing Someone back to life; it was God's act of raising the Man who had lived and died and celebrated.

Maybe this is why the first thing Jesus did after being resurrected was to throw another party. He met a couple of heartbroken disciples who weren't able to look up from the ground long enough to recognize that the One they were mourning was standing right in front of them. (See Luke 24.) Jesus broke bread and poured wine. And those of us who follow Him have been doing it ever since.

For the earliest Christians, celebration was not a way to avoid the pain of the world or to shut themselves off from the unpleasant parts of human existence. It was instead a recognition that the worst elements of the world—death, injustice, and oppression—weren't the final realities of our lives.

For Jesus, partying was an apologetic, a witness to an alternate way to face the world. What came to be known as the Love Feast by the earliest Christians was, in effect, a way of protesting the darkness. It was an invitation from Jesus-followers for everyone to join in. It was a recognition that God was like Jesus, and that meant that God was not against us; He was for us. And just as importantly, God was with us.

A few months ago, the church I (Jonathan) serve had a party for Martha. Martha had been in prison for more than a decade; then after she was released, she had to spend years on parole. On the day her parole finally ended, we threw a party to celebrate Martha's freedom. She was reentering society fully, and the church thought that was worth celebrating with cake and punch.

For an evening, people celebrated something really significant. There were tears and hugs and high-fives and junk food. But Martha's party had really started a few years earlier.

When she first entered prison, she was incredibly lonely. The other inmates received letters from friends and family, but Martha didn't have a support group. She was more than incarcerated—she was alone.

One day a prison chaplain suggested that she read the New Testament, mentioning that Paul's letters could be considered God's letters sent to Martha.

Then the chaplain gave Martha a Bible.

At first she ignored the chaplain's advice. Two-thousand-year-old letters couldn't replace notes from a friend. But eventually Martha picked up the Bible just to skim through it. When she did, one word caught her attention and eventually got her to read the whole Bible.

The word that stood out is found in the first verse of the third chapter of Paul's letter to Christians in Ephesus:

"I, Paul, the *prisoner* of Christ Jesus."

And the soul feels its worth.

11

Your Blessed Life Now

At a Jesus Party, the Tables Are Turned

> Even when they call us mad, when they call
> us subversives and communists and all the
> epithets they put on us, we know we only
> preach the subversive witness of the Beatitudes,
> which have turned everything upside down.
>
> —Archbishop Oscar Romero, a month before
>   he was assassinated for preaching the gospel

> Blessed are the cracked, for they shall let in
> the light.
>
> —Groucho Marx

A few years ago, the mayor of Abilene, Texas, invited me (Jonathan) to a banquet to hear Tony Campolo speak. Campolo has long been a role model for me and I was especially excited because I would have the chance to sit at the same table with him. For weeks I looked forward to it. I would casually bring it up to some of my friends, just to see the look of envy on their faces.

When the big day came, I showed up earlier than everyone else. I found the table that had a placeholder card with Tony's name on it, and I took the seat next to it. I had imagined that Tony and I would introduce ourselves and would instantly hit it off, perhaps share some life experiences. Maybe he would see something in me and ask me to go on tour with him to talk about following Jesus.

When someone tapped me on the shoulder, I presumed it was a server wanting to take drink orders. It wasn't. It was the mayor of Abilene. Turns out the invitation I had received did not include a seat at the table of honor. It turns out the head table had been overbooked. The mayor graciously apologized for the mistake, and I began the walk of shame to the back of the room.

Of course, I forgave the mayor. I know there's no use in holding on to resentment. That would only be petty. So I'll just write about it in a book.

At one point in his speech, Campolo said if you want to describe many American churches, you simply have to reverse the Beatitudes. The passages of Scripture where Jesus blesses all the wrong people. It was a sad commentary, and for most churches it was sadly accurate.

That's not to say Christians aren't familiar with the Beatitudes. But try to live in the power of the words for a week and your life may shatter.

There is a reason why we tend to reduce the Beatitudes to beautiful poetry rather than to let this passage challenge us. The words are counterintuitive, and frankly, absurd. Who could live like that?

Jesus is the only One who can fully live out the Beatitudes, but His followers are those who are committed to going all out to try. You cannot follow Jesus and ignore the Beatitudes (see Matthew 5). These words describe how Jesus lived, and following Him will lead us to do the same.

After all, the One who said, "Blessed are the poor" (verse 3) had no place to lay his head. The One who said, "Blessed are those who mourn" (verse 4) later wept in Gethsemane. The One who said, "Blessed are those who hunger and thirst" (verse 6) later asked for something to drink on the cross. For the rest of His life, Jesus practiced what He preached.

BANQUETS AND BEATITUDES

The word Jesus used for "blessing" is not easy to translate. It's the Greek word *makarios,* which means something like "fortunate" or "happy." It is a word the Greeks used when talking about something such as contentment, the kind of feeling you get when you know your place in the world. It's a word that describes your feeling when you find out the party is big enough for you too.[1]

If you read the four Gospels for the first time, you might think Jesus was either crazy or cruel. He specified a number of groups of people who He insisted are blessed. These are people for whom life has dealt a painful hand. Jesus was basically telling them, "Congratulations! The Kingdom of God belongs to you!" (see Matthew 5:1–12).

But if you keep reading, you eventually will realize that Jesus wasn't only preaching a mystery, He was issuing personal invitations. For the rest of His earthly life, Jesus *partied what He preached.*

In the first century there was a common assumption that if you were blessed by God, your life would look a certain way. And if you did not have the favor of God, your life would look another way. If you were healthy and wealthy, it was assumed that you were right with God, and if you were poor or sick, then it was taken as an indication that you had done something to anger God. This was the theology of Job's friends, and it's a way of thinking about God that is common today.

Turn on most popular television preachers, and you will hear that if you follow Jesus you should have a full bank account and no health problems. Our society, often our religion, says blessed are those who have a lot;

blessed are the strong; blessed are the powerful. But Jesus had just the opposite in mind.

Jesus told the poor, meek, persecuted people that their reward will be great in heaven. Westerners today tend to read that and think it means rewards to be received after our earthly life is over. But to a Jew, heaven is much more than just something that happens after you die. Heaven is where things are as God intends.

In God's economy, the unlikely people who are blessed are never seen as second class—just the opposite. They are blessed right now. This was revolutionary in first-century Judea, and it's just as revolutionary today.

And Jesus did not just say these counterintuitive words, He lived them out.

The book of Acts opens up with the writer Luke reminding his audience of all that Jesus had *done and taught*. That order in wording is important.

So often in today's Western versions of Christianity, we talk about whether the Bible or the Gospels are literally true. Was Jonah really swallowed by a big fish? Did Moses really hear a voice from within a bush that burned but never was consumed? Did the flood literally cover the earth entirely, even topping the highest mountains? The problem with these types of questions is that they seem to reduce the Bible to abstract theory, when Jesus is God's ultimate Word, and He wasn't just saying these things, He was actually *doing* them.

Jesus was not celebrated by the sinners and outcasts, or crucified by the religious leaders, just because of a disputed theory. He was killed for saying that God's blessing belongs to the least of these and then spending His life living out that reality. His opponents might be skilled at taking issue with something that He said, but it was an entirely different matter to try to overcome the effect of the life that He lived.

Jesus singled out every category of person that had been shunned by the elite of society, including the religious leaders and experts in the Law. In doing so, Jesus threw open the doors of God's Kingdom as wide as possible. Everyone, everywhere, is invited into God's Kingdom.

In a previous chapter we looked at the story in Luke 14 where Jesus went to a banquet and saw the way everyone was vying for a seat close to the place of honor. Jesus told his disciples not to make this mistake.

It's hard for most modern readers to grasp how revolutionary this story is. In Jesus's day strict social rules dictated how things went at a banquet. Pliny the Younger, a first-century Roman lawyer, wrote about a dining experience.

> Some very elegant dishes were served up to himself and a few
> more of the company; while those which were placed before the rest
> were cheap and paltry. He had apportioned in small flagons three
> different sorts of wine; but you are not to suppose it was that the
> guest might take their choice: on the contrary, that they might not
> choose at all. One was for himself and me; the next for his friends of
> lower order . . . ; and the third for his own freed-men and mine.[2]

Where you sat determined everything else about your banquet experience, from how much you would eat to how people viewed you as a person. The culture that Jesus was born into, and in which He lived and taught, was what is called an honor/shame culture.

The biggest commodity in that day was honor, and the worst thing that could happen was for you to bring shame upon yourself and your family. At a banquet, guests would situate themselves in relation to the person with the most prestige. The closer you were to the important person, the more honor was granted to you.

But Jesus opposed such a system. He didn't just warn His followers about pursuing seats of honor: He condemned the entire system! He asked pesky questions such as, Why are we drawn to the people everyone else says are important? Jesus continues to invite us to look in a different direction, to think differently about getting ahead. He challenges the accepted thinking on competing against our neighbors and taking advantage of others when it is to our advantage.

To resist the temptation to give in to such things benefits not just our neighbors but also ourselves.

A few years ago, I (Jonathan) was walking in downtown Fort Worth with my wife and a few friends. An elderly homeless man approached and asked for money for food. My friends and I had looked forward to that evening all week. We were celebrating a birthday, and we hadn't planned on having an additional guest. But one of my friends invited the man to come with us.

We had dinner in a swanky restaurant with the elderly man, whose name is LeVester (a French name that I assume means "The Vester"). What happened at that meal was gospel magic. LeVester was the life of the party. We went around the table and talked about our most embarrassing moments, and while I can't relate his story here, I assure you LeVester's tale won.

It's easy to think of this story as some middle-class people trying to give someone down on his luck a handout. But it was more than that. Something happened that night that altered the course of my life. I have eaten thousands of meals with good friends and good food, but that was a dinner I will never forget. At that meal, I saw a man transformed from being a bum to a human being.

JESUS COMES TO US IN A STRANGER

Maybe you have experienced the kind of joy that comes from finding Jesus in the stranger. I wish I was brave enough or selfless enough to experience it more. And let's be candid: this type of discipleship requires courage because it involves a certain kind of death.

Notice what Jesus said immediately after He gave people a new way to think about the customary banquet seating chart. Jesus talked about a new, expanded guest list.

> Then Jesus said to his host, "When you give a luncheon or dinner, do not invite your friends, your brothers or sisters, your relatives, or your rich neighbors; if you do, they may invite you back and so you will be repaid. But when you give a banquet, invite the poor, the crippled, the lame, the blind, and you will be blessed. Although they cannot repay you, you will be repaid at the resurrection of the righteous." (Luke 14:12–14)

In other words, be careful who you invite. Choose people who have so little standing in society, and so little money and influence, that they can't possibly help you advance your cause, your reputation, your career, or your bank account. According to the teachings of Jesus, the invited guests would include the lame, the blind, and the poor. Wherever a party is thrown that includes them, you will find the blessing of God.

And did you catch what Jesus said at the end? "You will be repaid at the resurrection of the righteous." This is the reason He gave for abandoning the accepted system of fighting for honor and prestige: God will repay us at the resurrection.

C. S. Lewis wrote about this idea:

> [What we are all after is fame] but not fame conferred by our fellow creatures—fame with God, approval or (I might say) "appreciation" by God. . . . [N]othing can eliminate from the parable the divine accolade, "Well done, thou good and faithful

servant." With that, a good deal of what I had been thinking all my life fell down like a house of cards. I suddenly remembered that no one can enter heaven except as a child; and nothing is so obvious in a child—not in a conceited child, but in a good child—as its great and undisguised pleasure in being praised. . . . It is written that we shall "stand before" Him, shall appear, shall be inspected. The promise of glory is the promise, almost incredible and only possible by the work of Christ, that some of us, that any of us who really chooses, shall actually survive that examination, shall find approval, shall please God. To please God . . . to be a real ingredient in the divine happiness . . . to be loved by God, not merely pitied, but delighted in as an artist delights in his work or a father in a son—it seems impossible, a weight or burden of glory which our thoughts can hardly sustain. But so it is. . . . For glory meant good report with God, acceptance by God, response, acknowledgment, and welcome into the heart of things. The door on which we have been knocking all our lives will open at last. . . . At present we are on the outside of the world, the wrong side of the door. . . . But all the leaves of the New Testament are rustling with the rumour that it will not always be so. Some day, God willing, we shall get in.[3]

This is what each one of us is after, even if we don't know it. And we will try to get it from everywhere and everyone we can. We'll work eighty-hour weeks to try to justify our existence through success in a career. We will try to get it from family or friends. We will fight to compare our achievements and character to others, hoping God grades on the curve. We will chase after fame and accolades not knowing they are only echoes of the deepest hunger of our souls: to be recognized and honored by God.

Here's a quick example. If you could get great accolades for doing something that wasn't the greatest good you could do, or get no credit at all but do the most good, which would you choose?

I often catch myself wanting to be known as a servant more than I want to serve. I want to be known as a kind and generous person more than I want to be kind and generous. We want to be recognized as doing the right thing more than we want to bother with doing the right thing.

Jesus said the resurrection is the key to how we can let go of that tendency. Because God is watching and one day, when heaven crashes into earth, God will set the world right. He will expose what we've done in our lives (both the good and the bad).

And Jesus has this notion that we will never feel the greatest sense of accomplishment until all we really need, by way of recognition, is "Well done!" from the One who made us. Most of what Jesus said makes no sense apart from the resurrection. Blessed are the meek? Blessed are the poor? These statements make no sense unless there is a day when God will give honor to such people.

This is why Jesus talked so much about the resurrection. Resurrection isn't just an abstract doctrine, and it's not some litmus test for whether a belief is orthodox or not. Resurrection means that the way things are now is not the way they always will be.

There is a reason the Sadducees, the most conservative (and wealthy and powerful) Jewish sect of Jesus's day, didn't believe in the resurrection. It is because people who find themselves on top don't like the idea of God turning the world upside down. And that is precisely what the resurrection means, and it's why Jesus had the courage to teach and to live out the Beatitudes.

Jesus is bringing God's future into the present. He's bringing heaven to earth. With every banquet Jesus attends, with every party that Jesus throws, He reminds us that God sees how the privileged guard their honor and compete against others as a way to protect what they have. He sees how we chase honor at the expense of the well-being of others, and Jesus makes it clear that God will do something about it.

Jesus does not tell us to avoid being ambitious; He does call into question the direction of our ambition. If we really believe the things Jesus said, there will be a day of resurrection where everything is turned upside down. In that moment, when it is apparent what Jesus's values are and how our values compare, which seat is the best one to be occupying? If God's reality is coming full-force to earth, which seat do you really want to pursue in this life?

In God's reality, those who are unemployed are blessed. So are addicts, those who are anxious, the mentally ill, the unpopular. Blessed is the person who is HIV positive, the person with a disability, the person who has very little in the way of worldly goods. If you match any of these descriptions, then congratulations. The Kingdom of God is wide open to you!

TURNING THE TABLES

Remember Tony Campolo's point at the beginning of this chapter? He said that to describe most American churches we simply have to invert the Beatitudes.

It seems to me that no one thinks of the church when we think of *happy hour*. Maybe this is because the kind of parties that Jesus hosted and participated in involved people that we go out of our way to avoid.

It has often been noted that Sunday-morning church assemblies are the most segregated times of the week, and we're not just segregated along ethnic and racial lines. We separate ourselves by socioeconomics, school districts, minor theological distinctions. We look down on churches who worship differently or have different methods for serving God and their neighbors.

This is not a new problem. In one of the earliest Christian documents we have, the apostle Paul gave believers involved in a new-church plant practical advice on everything from how to deal with disagreements to their sexuality. Then he got to the real heart of their problem. It was a problem similar to the banquet seating-chart issue.

These Christians had been celebrating the wrong things in the wrong way. An example is how they celebrated the Eucharist (which is derived from the Greek word for "thanksgiving").

> In the following directives I have no praise for you, *for your meetings do more harm than good.* In the first place, I hear that when you come together as a church, there are divisions among you, and to some extent I believe it. No doubt there have to be differences among you to show which of you have God's approval. So then, when you come together, it is not the Lord's Supper you eat, for when you are eating, some of you go ahead with your own private suppers. As a result, one person remains hungry and another gets drunk. Don't you have homes to eat and drink in? Or do you despise the church of God by humiliating those who have nothing? What shall I say to you? Shall I praise you? Certainly not in this matter!" (1 Corinthians 11:17–22)

Your church gatherings do more harm than good! This is one of the harshest things Paul ever wrote. He even dips into sarcasm to say, "Of course there need to be divisions among you! How else would you know who God approves of?"

Too often we go to assemblies that bear Jesus's name and behave exactly the way Jesus warned us not to. We divide up the world in ways that reinforce the status quo and current divisions among people. All the while we forget that Jesus is present in the stranger, *that Jesus is blessing all the wrong people and that if we are not spending time with strangers, we severely limit the time we spend with Jesus.*

A few years ago, I (Jonathan) read the words of an author who was serving in a Christian ministry for sex workers. The ministry tried to help people flee from an industry that is difficult to escape. The author wrote about sitting in a circle that included former and current sex workers. He asked them why they thought Jesus was so intentional about reaching out to prostitutes.

An awkward silence followed. Finally, one of the women said, in broken English, "[Other people have] someone to look down on. Not us. Our families, they feel shame of us. No mother nowhere looks at her little girl and says, 'Honey, when you grow up I want you be good prostitute.' . . . Believe me, we know how people feel about us. People call us names: whore, slut, hooker, harlot. We feel it too. We are at the bottom. And sometimes when you are at the low, you cry for help. So when Jesus comes, we respond. Maybe Jesus meant that."[4]

I have a hunch this woman is close to the heart of God.

A COMMUNITY OPEN FOR ALL

In most societies and institutions, we focus on the majority, developing a strategy to create a large tent for as many like-minded people as possible. But creating a big tent requires a strong center, and that inevitably leaves people out. It leaves some on the margins rather than being included with the majority.

But for Jesus, the people on the margins were the center of His ministry. The guests at a Jesus party were those who had been excluded by everyone else. They ate and drank and celebrated the divine favor of God, which is open to all and rejected only by the people who thought they could lay hold of it in some other way.

Jesus people gather every week to celebrate God's favor, which has been given generously to all the wrong people. We gather each week to carry on the kind of parties Jesus threw.

The Christians in ancient Corinth were celebrating, but not in the way of Jesus. When Paul criticized them for the way they observed communion—excluding from the meal some who were hungry—he reminded them of Jesus's words at the Last Supper: "Do this in remembrance of me" (1 Corinthians 11:24). In other words, celebrate communion without ever taking your eyes off Jesus and the way He celebrates.

When Jesus asked His followers to remember Him in the meal, what if Jesus wasn't referring to the steps taken in a ritual? What if Jesus was saying instead to organize your gatherings just like this one? Make sure you invite tax collectors, traitors, zealots, rough blue-collar workers, and loudmouths. And seat them all at the same table, indicating to them and everyone else that they are welcomed and cherished by God.

In the Kingdom of God the door of God's grace is opened so wide that no one is excluded. Think about why we call this good news. In God's Kingdom, the only people who are excluded are the ones who think they have better things to do.

In Jesus's parable of the wedding banquet, the people who had better things to do were important, busy, in-demand people. In other words, the ones who chose not to be included were successful, popular, admired people. This is a sobering truth indeed.

Maybe you heard about the bulletin from a couple of years back at Our Lady of Lourdes Catholic Community. This Denver parish made the news just for what was in its church bulletin. Here's how people were welcomed:

> We extend a special welcome to those who are single, married,
> divorced, gay, filthy rich, dirt poor, yo no habla Ingles. We extend

a special welcome to those who are crying newborns, those who are skinny as a rail or could afford to lose a few pounds. We welcome you here if you just woke up or just got out of jail. We extend a special welcome to those who are over 60 but not grown up yet, and to teenagers who are growing up too fast. We welcome soccer moms, NASCAR dads, starving artists, tree-huggers. We welcome those who are in recovery or still addicted. If you blew all your offering money at the dog track, you're welcome here. We offer a special welcome to those who think the earth is flat, work too hard, don't work, can't spell, or because grandma is in town and wanted to go to church. . . . We welcome those who are inked, pierced or both. We welcome tourists, seekers and doubters, bleeding hearts . . . and you!"[5]

There's something so open-armed about this welcome that you start to feel like they really mean it. They've worked hard to imagine all the different places that people come from when they approach God, and they want to make sure everyone knows that God's not surprised or put off by anyone's way of life.

But this kind of invitation does something even more for me. It speaks to the parts of me that I'm ashamed of, the ways I've failed and then tried to hide the failure. The million ways I pretend to have all my junk in order just so I can fit in. It says that even that part of me is welcome at this party.

And that kind of party, that sounds a bit like heaven.

Part 3

Life in the Light of Heaven

> As they watched, he was taken up and
> disappeared in a cloud. They stood there,
> staring into the empty sky. Suddenly two
> men appeared—in white robes! They said,
> "You Galileans!—why do you just stand
> here looking up at an empty sky?"
>
> —Acts 1:9–11 (MSG)

Have you noticed how much Jesus talks about heaven or the Kingdom of heaven? He wants us to get it, now, in this life. Jesus was not a Teacher who told us to wait for the good things after we die. He wants us to be involved in bringing the life of heaven to bear on earth, now, in this life.

His stories about heaven and the Kingdom of heaven are so down-to-earth that it's easy to miss their importance. Jesus told us that the Kingdom is like a pearl, a field, a wedding, a net full of fish, a seed. Books have been written about what these similes mean, but almost no one emphasizes the most obvious thing Jesus was doing.

Jesus wanted us to see that heaven is *like this world*. The common, everyday, tangible, normal things that we pass by all the time—those things are like heaven.

Heaven is more than life on earth, of course. But heaven is most certainly something like what we experience on earth. Or at least, it's very much like what the first humans experienced with God in an unobstructed relationship, on the earth God created so that life could flourish.

Think about what Jesus *didn't* say about heaven. In the Gospels, He never mentioned clouds or harps or angels blowing trumpets in a distant, future realm. Jesus just looked around at people and places and experiences in life. And He said, "Here it is."

If all this is true, if life today on this earth matters so much, then the question we need to answer is, now what?

12

It's About Time

The Difficulty of Waiting and the Power of Hope

> The future is the major time zone in which
> Christian faith has its being.
> — Teilhard de Chardin

> You can get addicted to a certain kind of
> sadness.
> — Gotye

Why did Jesus return to Galilee after He was raised from the dead? The common Jewish assumption back in the day was that when the Messiah came He was going to restore Jerusalem to its rightful epicenter of power. But Jesus didn't go to Jerusalem.

He could have, and it would have been awesome. Picture Jesus walking into the palace, looking Pilate in the eye, and saying: "Hey, remember me?"

But He didn't do that. Instead, He headed back to the region of Galilee. Opting for Galilee over Jerusalem is a little like choosing not to go to New York City in favor of returning to Sandusky. Natives of Galilee spoke with a regional accent, and the area had none of the glamour or sophistication of Jerusalem. We will return to this idea later. For now, it's important that we talk about *time*.

THE FIRST QUESTION REMAINS UNANSWERED

It is thought that the earliest of the sixty-six books of the Bible isn't Genesis; it's Job. This is the story of a faithful man who obeyed God and who lost everything except God. In just one day, this man lost all his children, his wealth, and his property.

As you read Job's story, just when you think things can't possibly get any worse, a new series of disasters shocks you. You can imagine what it was doing to Job. Death, destruction, boils, collapsed buildings, total loss. Job was left with no remaining earthly connections except some "friends" who excelled in giving him bad advice.

The book of Job can be summed up with one word: *why*.

The most primal question we all keep asking is not "Where did we come from?" but "Why is life the way it is?" We can't avoid wondering why the most tragic things keep happening to so many people.

One of my (Jonathan's) favorite authors, Philip Yancey, wrote a book on this very question. It's called *The Question That Won't Go Away: Why?*

The world can't escape the word *why*. If you wonder what the point is in asking "why?" stick around. The longer I live the more Job's story resonates with me. His story is a narrative that spells out our most primitive questions, asked in a thousand different ways and to a dozen different people.

And even for Job, who was more consistently faithful to God than any other major figure in the Old Testament, the question is never really answered. At least not by God.

In the story, plenty of other people have an answer, and they don't hesitate to share it with the suffering Job. But when Job finally takes his questions to God, God honors the questions by showing up. He always seems to do that when people suffer. God shows up.

But even that statement isn't entirely accurate. It's not that God shows up in response to suffering; He is always present, no matter our circumstances. But in the dust of Job's ordeal, God did entertain questions. Job wanted answers, just as you or I would, given the same situation. And that is when God flipped the script.

Job was eager to get his questions answered, finally, but God had questions for Job to answer. That's how it often works. We poke at Scripture, and it pokes back. Scripture teaches us it is okay to ask questions of God, but we need to be prepared for some questions to come back at us.

Here's what is most interesting: God's questions seemed to have nothing to do with the situation Job was in. God asked questions such as "Do you know when the mountain goats give birth? Do you watch when the doe bears her fawn? Do you count the months till they bear? Do you know the time they give birth?" (Job 39:1–2).

Or how about this one: "Who let the wild donkey go free? Who untied its ropes?" (verse 5).[1]

And then the Lord said this to Job:

The wings of the ostrich flap joyfully,
>   though they cannot compare with the wings and
>   feathers of the stork.
She lays her eggs on the ground
>   and lets them warm in the sand,
unmindful that a foot may crush them,
>   that some wild animal may trample them.

She treats her young harshly, as if they were not hers;
> she cares not that her labor was in vain,

for God did not endow her with wisdom
> or give her a share of good sense.

Yet when she spreads her feathers to run,
> she laughs at horse and rider. (Job 39:13–18)

I'm not sure what counseling course the Lord took, but this is not a strategy that I'm familiar with. No pastor or psychologist would approach a man in deep grief asking him to pay attention to an ostrich, taking special note of how stupid the animal is. It's almost as if God is acknowledging to Job that he has lost a lot, but he hasn't lost everything. God is still in charge of creation, and it is still good.

The story ends with Job never getting an answer to his question. In its place he gains a different perspective.

God could have told Job, "See, Satan the accuser and I were conducting a little experiment. I bet an awful lot on you to come through, Job. I trusted you to show the rest of creation something, and even though you didn't know it, all the heavens have been watching you to see how you'd respond."

God could have laid it all out for Job, but He didn't.

He could have told Job, "Don't worry, I'm going to make you a stirring example for suffering people everywhere. Your name will be synonymous with the virtue of patience. Millions will one day find great comfort in your story."

But God didn't say those things. The only reassurance God offered was the truth that God is God and Job isn't. And as much as I'd like to tell you more about that part of the story, this isn't a chapter about Job . . .

This is a chapter about *time*.

THE CHURCH HAS A DIFFERENT CALENDAR

Both of us come from a free-church tradition, which means we aren't as tied to the historic liturgy and traditions from older streams of Christianity. (We don't enforce a creed or use prayer books, for instance.). But one thing that Christians from a free-church tradition miss the most is the calendar of Christian history. Time matters, and the church calendar is one way we can become aware of and make the most of our time.

In the book of Leviticus, between detailed passages describing abominations and why Israelites shouldn't wear polyester, God commands the Israelites to set apart one day a year for their sins to be forgiven and one day a week to remember that they are no longer slaves. Then in Leviticus 23, God gives them detailed instructions on how they are to annually commemorate being rescued out of slavery by preparing a special meal. These are passages that many just skim over, but they are where we find two incredibly powerful ideas. First, our time matters. Second, the story we lay on top of our time matters.

The Bible—in nearly one thousand different places—addresses how we think about time. In fact, the Bible writers care just as much about time as the modern Western person, but in a very different way.

I doubt most people in America have a strong awareness of time as sacred. Or at least we don't think we do.

However, we intuitively recognize that certain parts of the year matter more, and we act accordingly. Tourists go to New England in October to enjoy autumn foliage. College students go to the Gulf Coast during spring break. Snow boarders travel to the mountain west in the winter to take advantage of the best powder. We are not strangers to the rhythms of creation.

But it's becoming more common for Christians to overlook, or even ignore, how our view of time shapes our lives and the way we view God. Aside from Christmas, family birthdays, a wedding anniversary, and Easter, Christians often deemphasize attempts to call attention to special days, festivals, holidays, and sacred observances. The Christian calendar frequently is thought of as little more than an anachronism, or worse, it is seen as a destructive tool in the hands of those who would limit a Christian's freedom to practice his faith according to the leading of the Holy Spirit.

But there is danger in not paying attention to the Christian calendar. The danger is that, in the name of spiritual liberty, we will orient our time around something other than God and His work in our lives. We will instead orient our days around spring break, the last day of the school year, tax day, Independence Day, or the Super Bowl.

We get the English word *holiday* from the idea of holy days. There are certain days and seasons that are different from others. They are days that are set apart to remind us that the Jewish/Christian faith is one that is rooted in history.

A holy day commemorates something significant that happened in the past. It acknowledges that God has been up to something all along, and He continues to work in miraculous and life-changing ways. He is active in our world and in our lives, and we must not minimize the importance of what He has done and is doing. We live in an enchanted world where God has been working all along. The Christian calendar helps us revisit those works of God in light of *time*.

We know intuitively that there is a time for joy and a time for tears. We have a deep-seated need for life to not just blend into one continuous stream of moments.

A couple of months ago, I (Jonathan) read a fascinating article in *The New York Times* about how people inside prison view time. As a former jail chaplain, I thought it was incredibly accurate. Inmates don't wear watches; they don't count time the way people on the outside do. They measure time in months, not minutes.[2]

The writer of the article had taught inmates for more than a decade. He learned from them to measure time in a different way. The inmates' method was to measure time by love and loss. Time wasn't just a series of to-do lists but a way of recounting meaning and determining future direction.

This is very much like the way the Bible talks about time.

The writer of Ecclesiastes wrote that time is God's way of helping us embrace our limitations. We will live and we will die, and the world will go on. So we should number our days because this is wisdom. Time is God's gift to us, which carries the idea that what we do with it is our gift back to God.

THE TIME OF OUR LIVES

We tend to orient our time around nature. From experience we know that one rotation of the earth begins and ends a day. Roughly ninety such days mark the beginning and end of a season. And one orbit of the earth around the sun constitutes three hundred sixty-five days, or a year. In addition, time has a far more personal meaning for all of us. On average we have seventy winters, seventy springs and summers, and seventy autumns. Such a passage of time, for many, marks the beginning and end of earthly life.

Due to the predictability and sequence of day and night, season following season, and weather patterns that correlate with seasons, we tend to view time in a linear fashion. D follows C follows B follows A. We find it difficult to imagine life that operates outside this scheme. Because of that, it seems to us that God is slow to act, slow to answer, and slow to show up when we need Him most.

How many more times does the earth have to orbit the sun before God finally does something? And why—if all it takes is for God to speak a word—doesn't He just go ahead and set things right?

If you have asked such questions, you are far from the first one.

The Israelites were held in slavery for more than four hundred years before God showed up in a burning bush. Lazarus was dead for four days before Jesus decided it was time for a road trip. Most of the people Jesus healed had been sick most of their lives. We could conclude that God does not view time the way we do.

A few decades after Jesus's resurrection, a group started saying Jesus wasn't going to come back to earth. This was a time issue, or more accurately, a perception-of-time issue. The apostle Peter sought to set the record straight:

> By the same word the present heavens and earth are reserved for
> fire, being kept for the day of judgment and destruction of the
> ungodly. But do not forget this one thing, dear friends: With the
> Lord a day is like a thousand years, and a thousand years are like a
> day. The Lord is not slow in keeping his promise, as some under-
> stand slowness. Instead he is patient with you, not wanting anyone
> to perish, but everyone to come to repentance. (2 Peter 3:7–9)

It's important to note that the fire mentioned by Peter is not a reference to any intention on God's part to destroy the world. Notice that Peter told this story in the context of Noah's flood. It was a flood that didn't destroy the world but judged and refined it. Remember, God's judgment is not meant to destroy; instead it is a gift to us.

Peter is telling us to rest assured that God will do something like that again. The world will be set right one day, but keep in mind that God doesn't think of time like we do.

God is outside time, because He made the very things we mark time with. How can the One who created the solar system be bound by how many times the earth orbits the sun? But that does not mean that He is not deeply involved in what is happening. One day God will redeem everything that happens inside of time.

But not yet.

Paul wrote that we should grieve but with hope. It sounds like a great sentiment, but too often Christians have used it to avoid the pain of the moment. We rush to talk about heaven and resurrection. We rush to hope as a way to soften the pain of grief. And the opposite is equally true: some of us feel at home in grief, but rarely catch glimpses of hope.

Grieve with hope? What does that look like?

In the first church that I (Jonathan) worked at, after a few months I got involved in an intergenerational small group. That is where I met a sweet couple named Pam and Jerry Gilbreath.

They had been married for decades, and they were the kind of spouses who could finish each other's sentences. They gave the young people in our group everything from marriage advice to spiritual direction to casserole recipes.

And then one day Jerry wasn't feeling well. Pam rushed him to the hospital, but just a few days later Jerry died. Something was lost for Pam that day, and it hasn't been entirely set right even years later. She has learned what life looks like with this new normal, but there is a sadness in her eyes. She is wise enough to not try to hide it.

But the greater the loss, the greater the joy when it's restored.

A few years ago, I met Lil and Arnold Pitchford. They are hands-down the most romantic couple I've ever known. But if you knew Arnold, you wouldn't expect romantic.

In 2009, he was wrangling cattle on his ranch and one of the bulls charged him. Arnold is a seventy-year-old man, but no one has told him that. When the bull charged Arnold, it hit him full force in the face, knocking him over, and then ran back over him for good measure. Not one to stay down, Arnold got right back up and wrestled the bull into a trailer and then Lil drove him to the Emergency Room. As the doctors were patching him up, Arnold spit out a tooth. I kid you not, it was the bull's tooth!

But as tough as he was on the outside, Arnold was twice as kind and in love with Lil on the inside. A few months after he wrestled a bull, Arnold was back working on the ranch. That's when he saw Lil's car come speeding toward where he was working. She stopped the car and rushed to Arnold's side. "The doctor just diagnosed me with stage-four cancer," she said. "I don't have long."

Arnold did what, by then, was his first instinct. He leaned down and kissed Lil on the forehead. He told her, "You'll be the prettiest baldheaded girl in the state of Texas." And to him, she was. For two more years I saw a man love a woman fully. She opened like a flower to him. And then finally and cruelly, cancer took Lil from Arnold.

Not a day goes by that he doesn't write her a poem or tell someone her story. And he waits. He waits with great loss.

But the greater the loss, the greater the joy when it's restored.

A few years ago I (Jonathan) had a friend who became pregnant unexpectedly. The couple had thought their child-bearing years were behind them, and the wife was seven months pregnant before they discovered her condition could not be attributed to indigestion. A couple of months later, their healthy baby girl was born.

And ten days later the baby died.

Since I was the only pastor they knew, they asked me to come and help them say good-bye to their little girl. I had never officiated at the funeral of an infant before, so I asked one of my mentors for advice. He recommended that I should go to the funeral home before anyone else got there and try to acclimate myself to the shock of seeing such a tiny coffin.

I did, and I found myself overwhelmed with sadness. What do you say in the face of such grief?

What words do justice when it feels like there no such thing as justice?

Brené Brown the professor of sociology famous for her powerful TED talk on vulnerability, said in an interview that upon her return to church she had assumed that the church would help to numb the pain that comes with life. But she discovered that the church was more like a midwife, one that helped you sit through the pain and bear it.[3]

I think this is what Paul was getting at when he wrote about the idea of grief and hope (see 1 Thessalonians 4:13–18). The two go together because the greater the grief, the greater the hope.

The longer something is lost the greater the joy when it's found.

The longer one is sick, the greater the joy when you recover.

The longer the absence, the greater the joy when lovers are reunited.

The promise of Scripture is that one day all things will be restored. All of us have suffered loss and sadness and sickness and displacement. All of us will come face-to-face with life on earth as God created it in the beginning. The hope is great because our grief is great.

Lil will once again hold hands with the man who misses her so much.

Parents will never again have to bury their children.

The prophet Isaiah saw this day coming:

Never again will there be in it
    an infant who lives but a few days,
    or an old man who does not live out his years;

the one who dies at a hundred
will be thought a mere child;
the one who fails to reach a hundred
will be considered accursed.
They will build houses and dwell in them;
they will plant vineyards and eat their fruit.
(Isaiah 65:20–21)

This is what it means to grieve with hope. You live with loss—and with the expectation that God will give it all back. The things that we lose or have lost in the past can be signposts pointing to a time of great restoration.

I won't try to defend God and His sense of timing. He doesn't need me or anyone else to make excuses for Him. But here is the honest truth from my standpoint. Of all the reasons not to believe in God, this is the one I understand the best: If God is good, then why do I keep going to funerals? Why does evil seem to be on the increase? Why is there so much suffering?

I understand those questions. I have asked them myself. But there is the other side to consider. The argument that has to be considered, before you write God off, relates to the reality of beauty and good. There are moments when our hearts swell at a sunrise, at the sound of a child's laughter, or at the sight of birds flying overhead. We are overwhelmed with gratitude when we get a hug at a time when that is exactly what we needed. A dad swings his little girl at a playground, and it feels like someone is standing on your chest. You don't have to know the dad or the child; just the sight of love and happiness, of people enjoying life and being together, that is goodness and beauty.

There has to be point to all this.

What do you do with the moments when you are overwhelmed, not by loss, but by the wonder of life?

Which brings us back to God's seeming nonanswers to Job.

It's easy to see all that is bad, but when you are trying to write off God, He forces you to notice the good. Sure, it's an incomplete good. We love someone and that person dies. We see beautiful flowers growing, then in a few weeks they dry up and turn brown. But beauty is there, and it acts as a signpost pointing to another time, a time in which God will fill the earth. We will be surrounded by love and good and beauty, and those things will never fade.

This is the vision that sustained the early Christians in the face of unbearable suffering. They knew that God would one day give it all back.

Here is how Paul presented this notion when he wrote to Christians in Rome: "I consider that our present sufferings are not worth comparing with the glory that will be revealed in us" (Romans 8:18). The sufferings are *not worth comparing* to the glory that will be revealed in us.

Paul had been beaten five times, shipwrecked three times, beaten with rods three times, stoned once, and thrown in jail too many times to count. Paul wrote that his suffering would be nothing more than a footnote in history because he was sustained by a vision of a day when God will give it all back.

None of this is meant to make light of suffering. I have so many questions. But the Christian hope says that the God who is above time is also able to redeem what happens in our time.

A few years ago, I read an article about heaven written by Joni Eareckson Tada. Joni is a well-known Christian author and speaker who is a quadriplegic. When she was young, she had an accident that rendered most of her body paralyzed. She had to learn to discern mentally her blood pressure, in case she was bleeding and not aware of it. Joni speaks all over the country about the way that tragedy has shaped her life and how she finds God with her in it, and Joni talks a lot about the age to come.

Joni wrote that she imagines what the first few moments of heaven will be like. This is how she described the scene:

> The good things in this life are only omens and foreshadowing of more glorious, grand, great things to burst on the scene when we walk into the other side of eternity. For one thing, the Bible assures us that we're going to have new bodies. First Corinthians, chapter 15, read it sometime for some encouragement. We learn there that one day we will have new hands, new legs that will walk, new hearts, new minds.
>
> I can't wait for the day when I'm given my brand new glorified body. I'm going to stand up, stretch, dance, kick, do aerobics, comb my own hair, blow my own nose, and what is so poignant is that I'll finally be able to wipe my own tears, but I won't need to, because the Bible tells us in the book of Revelation that God will personally wipe away every tear.[4]

As you read Joni's work or listen to her story, you get a sense that she's waiting for something with a greater anticipation than other people, even those of us who believe the exact same things. Maybe this is what Jesus meant when He said that in the kingdom of heaven the last will be first. Joni's life is not enviable, and her suffering is nothing to gloss over, but at the Restoration of all things, her joy will be greater than mine, because she will have more given back to her.

This is the great Christian hope that has allowed millions of Jesus followers to wait patiently even in the middle of great pain, because the longer the grief, the greater the joy when finally it is abated. The greater the sorrow, the greater the joy when sorrow ceases. The greater the loss, the greater the restoration when God brings it into being in full.

Which brings us back to the matter of Jesus, when He returned to Galilee following His resurrection. He chose not to go to Jerusalem, the acknowledged center of religion and trade. I think He went to Galilee because that's where the disciples, His people, were. God raised Jesus from the dead, but not to make headlines or to shock Jesus's enemies in Jerusalem. Rather, God raised His Son from the dead for *us*.

Jesus came back to Galilee to show God's people that what His Father did for Him, He will one day do for all of us. There will be a day when everything changes, when the soon becomes now, when the future becomes present, when all wrongs are righted.

The glory of God will fill the earth, and the lion will lie down with the lamb. Death will die and all of creation will join in the celebration of God's making all things new. Branches will wave, flowers will grow, waves will roar, and groans will cease.

This kind of restoration is for all creation, everything that God made. All of creation will join with the Creator saying . . .

It's about time.

How to Lose the Fear of Failure

Fears and Perfectionism Keep Us from Joining Jesus's Celebration

> I believe that the desire to please you [God]
> does, in fact, please you. . . . And I know
> that . . . you will lead me by the right road
> though I may know nothing about it.
> Therefore. . . . I will not fear, for you are ever
> with me, and you will never leave me to face
> my perils alone.
>
> — A prayer of Thomas Merton

Phobias are not the same as pet peeves. The latter simply have the potential to drive us nuts. Being in the presence of a fingernail biter, a loud cell-phone talker, or a gum smacker may make you want to scream. Those are pet peeves, not phobias. I don't know anyone who responds to such annoyances with a paralyzing fear. Even if you argue that open-mouthed ice-chomping can land the offender in the eternal pit of weeping and gnashing of teeth, it's still a pet peeve, not a phobia.

Phobias interfere with life and cause deep personal distress. They alter moods and lifestyles. They can have a major impact on relationships. Phobias also can change how we think about time, and they can prevent us from wanting to join in the party that Jesus invites us to.

According to the National Institute of Mental Health, 6.3 million Americans have been clinically diagnosed with a phobia. Some are common and won't come as a surprise. The top three phobias are (1) glossophobia, the fear of speaking; (2) necrophobia, the fear of death; and (3) arachnophobia, the fear of spiders.[1]

Other phobias are comical. Did you know there is a named phobia for people who fear having company in their home? It's called anthropophobia. Every Thanksgiving and Christmas there is a reaction to syngenesophobia, a fear of relatives. Aulophobia is a fear of flutes, and one of the newest classified phobias is nomophobia, and it is spreading like a flu epidemic. It affects people who are fearful of losing cell-phone contact. It's the feeling of driving on the interstate, seeing No Service in the top left-hand corner of your phone, and then beginning to hyperventilate as if a major organ is not working correctly—all because you may miss an incoming text message.

I (Josh) have friends who suffer from aerophobia, a fear of flying. I've had flying experiences that could have given me this phobia. A couple of years ago I was on an eleven-hour flight from Johannesburg to London. As they were closing the doors on the plane, I noticed that the only three vacant seats were next to me. This is good news if you're on a one-hour flight, but it's *great news* if you're on an eleven-hour flight. However, before we were pushed back from the passenger gangway, the aircraft's door opened and onto the plane walked a mother with four small children. They sat next to me.

As a father of two young boys, I have a ton of compassion for young parents. Flying with children is a daunting task, so I did everything I could to help them get situated. The first four hours were uneventful.

Then it all changed. One of the small children puked. Everywhere. Some of it landed on my foot . . . I was wearing flip-flops. I began to hyperventilate.

The kid had infringed on a phobia that has haunted me for decades. It's the fear of vomiting. It has a name: emetophobia. I do not automatically throw up when others throw up. I just despise them for a really long time. Being in the presence of—or even just hearing about—a vomiting person triggers my phobia.

I am better now because I have experience being a dad, but it's still a fear that alters my attitude. Even when a friend from hundreds of miles away informs me in a phone conversation that someone in his family has the stomach bug, I hang up the phone and wash my hands immediately. My wife laughs. I don't. I begin to worry that the bug is inside me.

Did you know that 60 percent of phobias will never actually take place? Ninety percent of the things we fear are considered to be insignificant issues. And 88 percent of things feared are in relation to our health and will never come to pass.[2] Yet we live in a culture that is obsessed with fear.

Fear has become a valuable tool in the hands of news outlets, political campaigns, and even churches. Fear manipulates and controls people, influencing outcomes.

Many people live in fear of worst-case scenarios. What if the chandelier falls? What if all five locks on the front door aren't in a locked position when we head off to bed?

We are fearful because we have heard stories and we've watched movies and we've listened to country music. Bad things happen, and most of the time it has nothing to do with our unwise choices or self-destructive behavior. We fear things because we have children and want them to be safe, or because we have been hurt in the past and never want to be hurt again.

Fear isn't always negative. It keeps us on our toes. It teaches us to be people of caution. And sometimes these things are good.

But fear is not good when it haunts our families and triggers unhealthy decisions. It has penetrated the life of the church, keeping us from embracing risky faith. Fear can paralyze decision making that would draw us deeper into the heart and mission of God. There is a reason the command "Do not be afraid" shows up more than any other command in Scripture.

There is a phobia that has the power to paralyze the church as well as the culture of the twenty-first century. It's called atychiphobia, a fear of failure. This is closely connected to the fear of letting people down and being obsessed with pleasing people. It is described as an extreme, irrational fear.

It's easy to say we don't care what people think of us, but in our heart of hearts we do. We want to be accepted; we want people to think well of us. I have a friend who is a pastor. His addiction to people-pleasing led him into a twelve-step program. It can become a form of idolatry, and it can cripple the local church. Kingdom people who take risks for the gospel must conquer their need to hear applause.

As destructive and dissatisfying as people-pleasing can be, atychiphobia is more than an irrational drive to be a people pleaser. It is the abnormal, unwarranted, persistent fear of failure. It leads to a constricted way of life, and it has a profound impact on one's willingness to engage in certain activities.

There is real danger here for followers of Jesus. Failure can loom so large that Christians choose to avoid all risks. They may fear failure so much that they choose to not take a risk again. Their default setting in life will be to play it safe no matter what. This has a profound and stifling impact on discipleship, evangelism, loving neighbors, creating community, fostering environments for authenticity, and living out the Great Commission and the Great Commandment.

The fear of failure causes people to hold back and to avoid trying anything they are not certain they can do perfectly. People who suffer from atychiphobia refuse to take a risk unless they are assured in advance that they can pull things off to perfection. That, of course, removes all risk from the equation.

This fear helps explain why so many Christians are locked in homogeneous communities. In most congregations you will see very little ethnic diversity. Further, churches often organize ministries and activities in ways that segregate seniors from younger members, married persons from singles, youth from adults, and even men from women. It is rare to hear anyone raise serious questions that can lead to fruitful discussion and learning. The emphasis instead focuses on fitting in and being just like everyone else. Such uniformity might make people feel safe and comfortable, but it is the opposite of risky faith.

The sense of safety that comes with constantly pleasing people insulates us from seeing how creative and diverse God is.

You might read on a church website that the congregation welcomes people just as they are. But the unstated fine print lists exceptions. All are welcome (except single mothers, cohabitating couples, those showing symptoms of substance abuse, anyone dressed like a gang banger or biker or sex worker, same-gendered couples, women wearing shorts, those who don't speak English, and undocumented immigrants).

The fear of people who aren't like us keeps us separate from our neighbors. We set up parallel structures, such as alternate school proms, homeschool collectives for gym class and field trips, church softball leagues, and other efforts that duplicate what our neighbors are involved in. When we could be joining our neighbors in park district sports and community work days and block parties, we stay busy doing the same types of things but with people who remind us of ourselves.

For many Christians, voluntary isolation is a life commitment. We segregate our children from other children by keeping our kids out of public school. We justify it by saying that twelve humans wearing judicial robes tossed God out of public education. This is fear, although few of us realize it. God is Creator of the universe, and He never will take His cues from the US Supreme Court. God doesn't need anyone's permission to enter into any place in the universe, much less a public school classroom.

Fear can keep us from raising our children to believe they have something great to offer to the world.

Can you see how paralyzing and detrimental this is for the local church? If heaven really is invading earth, if Kingdom parties are as inclusive and welcoming as we claim them to be, how do our fear-limited lives serve as a witness to others? How can our isolation be taken as an open invitation to others to join the celebrations endorsed by heaven?

PERFECT LOVE DRIVES OUT FEAR

"Do not let your hearts be troubled. You believe in God; believe also in me" (John 14:1). Jesus spoke these words to His followers. A few moments later He declared Himself to be "the way and the truth and the life" (verse 6). But a few moments prior, He predicted Peter's denial. That's a lot happening in the span of sixty seconds' worth of words.

Remove the chapter break (which was added hundreds of years later) and listen again to what Jesus said:

> Simon Peter asked him, "Lord, where are you going?"
> Jesus replied, "Where I am going, you cannot follow now, but you will follow later."

Peter asked, "Lord, why can't I follow you now? I will lay
down my life for you."

Then Jesus answered, "Will you really lay down your life for
me? Very truly I tell you, before the rooster crows, you will
disown me three times!

Do not let your hearts be troubled. You believe in God;
believe also in me." (John 13:36–14:1)

Immediately after Jesus predicted Peter's denial, He said, "Do not let
your hearts be troubled." It's as if the message is this: "After you fail Me,
Peter, redemption will be able to capture you, because I am still the Way,
Truth, and Life." The same message applies to you and to me.

Jesus's words are reassuring for those of us who have let God down,
or have misrepresented Him by what we have done and failed to do.

Peter would need these words as he reflected on his denial of Christ.
The words of Jesus would mean more to Peter after his betrayal than they
meant in the upper room. His guilt over denying Jesus three times could
easily have prevented Peter from ever again taking a risk as a follower of
Christ.

He could struggle with a renewed fear of failure. We all know how it
works. There are so many things that need to be done, but we are afraid
of either failing at the tasks or letting people down as we try to carry out
the tasks. We end up not doing what we know we're supposed to do.

After Peter betrayed Jesus, we read in the Gospel of John that Peter
left a fishing boat to be next to Jesus. They reunite over a fish fry on the
shore. Surely, there were a lot of questions Jesus could have asked, and
maybe should have asked, this particular disciple.

"Why did you deny Me three times, Peter?"

"Are you sorry?"

"How depressed have you been?"

"What are you willing to do to show Me that you really do care about all the things I taught you?"

"Do you promise never to fail again, Peter?"

If we had been betrayed by someone who for three years had been a constant, trusted companion, we might have felt justified in asking these questions. However, Jesus didn't reprimand or question Peter, or even bring up the past. He simply asked one question:

"Do you love me?" (John 21:15).

The central question following abandonment and betrayal had to do with loving Jesus. How appropriate.

The apostle John would later make this claim: "There is no fear in love. But perfect love drives out fear" (1 John 4:18). It takes guts to make that claim. Think about it. If perfect love drives out fear, what are the things that need to be driven out of your life? What needs to be driven out of the life of the church? The fear of failing at a new ministry initiative, or the obsession with trying to keep a dozen people happy? These are not concerns that ever directed Jesus's decision making. He taught His followers differently.

If heaven is the place of unending devotion to God and where all things are made right, then we know the world needs heaven, not an escape plan. We need to engage this world as if right now matters for eternity. Because it does.

The fear of failure gets in the way of the Jesus party. And for many congregations, fear prevents throwing a party altogether. Someone said to me, "When my trust in God is greater than my fear of the unknown, I will be able to rest, even though I don't have a clue what will greet me around the corner."

Kayci and I do our best to make our boys aware of injustice in the world, both locally and globally. We want to teach them to believe that they have something valuable to offer. Since our boys began to talk, their lips have prayed over Memphis, the rich, and the poor. We want homogeneity to stand out to them as being nonnormative, rather than the preferred reality.

Kayci usually carries bottles of water and peanut-butter crackers in the car to give to people standing on street corners. Our boys have grown up watching her do this, and now they point out people who are at the side of a street holding a cardboard sign.

One day they came to a stop at a red light, and there was a man on the corner. Unfortunately, Kayci had given away all her bottled water and peanut-butter crackers. Truitt and Noah began to say, "Mom, give him something. Help him. Do something." When Kayci remained silent, they took their game to another level. "Mom, don't you love Jesus?" It can be challenging when your children become voices for the Kingdom.

Since they were all in the car, Kayci employed a standard parenting technique. She turned up the radio.

I'm guilty of the same thing, but in a variety of situations. Instead of turning up the sound for the party, I turn up the sound of fear, keeping myself and sometimes others from joining the party. We can easily cheat ourselves out of celebrating because we are committed to illusions of safety and protection.

No matter how much we avoid risk and give in to fear, nothing can change what God is doing and what He will do when heaven crashes to earth. The sounds of the Kingdom coming into this world will drown out all sounds made by fear.

Perfect love drives out fear, and when that happens, we can't help but celebrate.

What Comes Next?

Your View of Tomorrow Determines How You Live Today

> "If you're a city planner, there is a New Jerusalem. If you're a lawyer there will be a time of perfect righteousness and justice".... The way we view the not yet will inevitably impact the way we respond in the here and now.
>
> — Tim Keller

Typically it happens somewhere around cruising altitude. We're all buckled in and my seatmate will turn to me (Jonathan) and ask what my job is. Immediately, when I mention I'm a pastor, the atmosphere changes.

If the person has a religious background, he might try to remember what he has said up to this point. He wonders if he might have offended me. If he has a *really* religious background, he might be grateful that I'm sitting next to him. He might even mention, from 33,000 feet, that he feels safe now. As if God prevents turbulence based on the clergy-laity passenger ratio on each commercial flight. (A cursory look at the book of Acts makes you think that ministers are anything but safe travel buddies.)

A lot of times people shut down the conversation all together because they think the next words out of my mouth will be, "Have you accepted Jesus as your Lord and Savior?"

I have noticed, though, that more and more people ask something like "Why do you do that? That seems like a waste of a perfectly good, you know, life." I love that question. Behind it lies the idea that the story of God doesn't have a lot to do with this world and this time. The irony is that the story of God taught us to ask questions just like that one.

Working with God

I (Jonathan) go to church with a guy I call Dr. Tom. Tom became a Christian well into his adult life. He was getting his PhD in biology when his wife asked him to go to church with her. Most of what Tom knew of Jesus was that Jesus landed on the wrong side of science at the Scopes Monkey Trial, but he loved his wife so he tried attending church.

Tom was surprised to find some of his colleagues there. He knew them to be people who were intellectually curious about the way the world works. It seemed, however, that they hadn't had to check their brains at the door to follow Jesus.

Once Dr. Tom heard the story of Jesus, he found Jesus so compelling that he decided to follow Him. He did this not in spite of his vocation, but actually through it. Today Dr. Tom is a biology professor at a liberal arts college. He recently discovered and named a new species of mammals in Ecuador. Every class he teaches he opens by saying something like "In the beginning, God asked people to name the animals. Some things never change."

Central to being human is the idea of a vocation (which is derived from a Latin word that means "calling"). We all have a sense that we ought to do something with our lives. We typically reduce that to mean we should find a way to earn an income, but the Scriptures have a different idea about what vocation means. That idea goes all the way back to the beginning of history.

From the beginning, God created the world and wanted humanity to engage *with Him* in significant ways in developing that creation. The Hebrew word for this concept is *mitzvoth,* a reference to partnership with God. We translate this word into English as "commandments" or "good works." It's not that God can't get His work done without partners, but He strongly prefers to work in partnership.

Jewish scholar Abraham Herschel said one of the worst consequences of sin's entering the world is that it prevented people from partnering with God. Adam and Eve interrupted their partnership with God in Genesis 3. That is when the relationship humanity has to its work changed. Before, humans lived in a garden. Now the soil has changed; the ground is filled with thorns and thistles.

The Bible has a lot to say about God's people working. This is an important but frequently neglected point.

RETURN TO A WORKING EDEN

Isaiah, when Israel was about to return from exile to Babylon, painted a picture for the Israelites about what kind of life God was inviting them into. Using the image of a feast, he invited them to "delight in the richest of fare" (Isaiah 55:1–2).

The word Isaiah used for delight is the word *Eden.* It's a reference to restoration, a return to what God originally intended for the world. Isaiah pointed out that in this new kind of life there would be no thorns and thistles—a reversal of the curse of Genesis 3. In the future, God would replace thorns with pines and myrtles. Isaiah went on to describe the new heavens and new earth (see 55:12–13).

> They will build houses and dwell in them;
>> they will plant vineyards and eat their fruit.
> No longer will they build houses and others live in them,
>> or plant and others eat.
> For as the days of a tree,
>> so will be the days of my people;
> my chosen ones will long enjoy
>> the work of their hands.
> They will not labor in vain. (Isaiah 65:21–23)

This passage has two reference points. First, Isaiah was writing to people who were about to return from exile to the land of Israel. So returning to the land God promised is one meaning. But the promises run even deeper.

It's a vision for God's dream of the universe, and according to Isaiah, in the new heavens and new earth people will build houses and plant vineyards, and their works will no longer be in vain.[1]

The Age to Come, if we are to believe Isaiah's vision, is a restored, renewed earth. And in that renewed heaven and earth, we will partner with God and with one another. We will work, and it will be a joy—productive, meaningful, and fulfilling. Finally, our work will be free from the curse.

Sometimes I hear people talk about heaven like it's a retirement home. But that runs counter to the reason God created you. Is there something you do that every time you engage in it you think, *I could do this forever?* Chances are, you just might.

A MILLION KINDS OF MINISTRY

Of all the churches Paul addressed in his letters, the congregation in ancient Corinth was most entrenched in Greek philosophy. Paul wanted them to be clear on the Resurrection and its implications, and oddly enough, one of the instructions he gave them was to stay in the same situation they were in when they first came to faith. To put it another way, they were to stay where they were when they were called by God (see 1 Corinthians 7:17).

Paul gave this advice because he was a Jew. He knew the story of a God who creates and calls His people to be co-creators. Paul knew that the first person the Bible describes as being filled with the Spirit is a guy named Bezalel. He was not a priest, king, or apostle. He was a skilled craftsman, the Bob Vila of the Old Testament.

Dozens of people have told me (Jonathan), "I don't think I'm pleasing God with my life. I'm thinking about getting into ministry." I wish I had told every one of them: "Maybe you already are."

Sometimes we get the idea that the really spiritual people are the ones who work at a church or a nonprofit. But the majority of stories in Scripture don't mention God's working through Levites or priests. Far more often the stories involve accountants, trumpet players, and carpenters.

Jesus could see that such people would be valuable to the Kingdom of God. It's time for us to gain some of the same vision. Paul didn't share the common Greek view of the soul and the flesh; he saw no division between sacred and secular work because God came in the flesh and worked as a carpenter.

This is a theme that has been largely neglected. In a letter that Paul wrote to the Christians in Thessalonica, he mentioned that he was a worker (see 2 Thessalonians 3:7–9). He went on to explain how the people should view their own work. Paul understood work.

He had been a prominent rabbi working in a capacity designed to help protect the beliefs and practices of Judaism. He was like a religious bounty hunter, tracking down those who were preaching the message of Jesus. But in the context of first-century Judea, he was in ministry. Then he met the risen Jesus and Paul became the world's most successful missionary. He also was a tent maker.

Paul did not require the financial support of the churches he planted; he worked on the side to provide for his financial needs. In his writing, he often mentioned work, the Kingdom, and glory. He wanted Christians to understand that their work should be shaped by the focus of their hope.

In the middle of his first letter sent to Christians at Thessalonica, Paul wrote some of the most profound, pastoral words of his career.

> We urge you, brothers and sisters, . . . to make it your ambition to
> lead a quiet life: You should mind your own business and work
> with your hands, just as we told you, so that your daily life may
> win the respect of outsiders and so that you will not be dependent
> on anybody. (1 Thessalonians 4:10–12)

Paul's work is largely responsible for Christian belief and teachings going beyond Palestine to spread around the world. But he never encouraged Christians to change vocations by leaving their trade to enter full-time ministry. Neither did he urge them to try to make a dent in the universe.

Instead, he told the Christians in Thessalonica to make it their ambition to lead quiet lives, to work hard, and to win over outsiders by the quality of their lives. Put another way, they were to be productive members of their community, good neighbors, good parents, and good students. Paul knew that over the long haul, the Jesus story had a better chance of being heard when it was told by people living respectable, productive, subtle lives.

That's the way the Kingdom of God works.

These days it is en vogue to critique the church's past, pointing out especially things the church has done wrong. But Christian history is filled with roses, not just thorns. The church has established hospitals, orphanages, libraries, and universities. Capuchin monks gave the world the cappuccino, and Irish monks saved civilization.

A cursory look at Christian history reveals that the world has been fundamentally altered by men and women following Jesus in community and trying to serve the world. The world was changed by Jesus-followers, but you probably don't know many of their names.

You might know saints such as Augustine and Francis, or reformers like Martin Luther and John Calvin. But for the most part the world has been changed and served by a cloud of largely anonymous witnesses who believed they could best serve the Lord by quietly serving their neighbor.

That's what Paul was getting at.

RESURRECTION, NOT RAPTURE, IS THE REAL R WORD

A few verses later, Paul makes a well-known reference to Christians meeting Jesus in the air (see 1 Thessalonians 4:17). This is an unexpected departure from his earlier instructions to work hard, be a good friend and neighbor, and lead a quiet life. Suddenly, Paul is writing about flying to heaven. Up to this point, his letter had a clear *earthly* purpose. But now the talk shifts to leaving earth for heaven. Or does it?

Much of Western Christianity over the past century has interpreted this passage to mean we just have to hold on, waiting out our time on earth until God beams us out of here to some celestial place just past the Hubble Space Telescope. Many of the problems facing Western Christianity hang on this one passage. We believe Christians have been reading into Paul's actual meaning. Out of the misunderstanding, Christians have created a theology of despair and escapism.[2]

Anytime a single Bible passage (or verse) represents the one lens that shapes a theology, you should be suspicious. If too much weight is given to an interpretation that varies from the rest of Scripture, be on your guard.

The first Christians who received Paul's letter would have known exactly what this passage meant. These people lived in Thessaloniki, an area wracked by earthquakes. Their city had been destroyed and a rebuilding project had to be undertaken. Caesar had heard about the destruction, and he sent FEMA-like resources to rebuild it.

After a while he sent word that he wanted to visit and see what they had done with his resources. When the emperor arrived, they blew a trumpet and one historian wrote that the entire city came out to welcome him. Then they returned to the village to show Caesar what they had done with his money.

Paul drew on this event when he wrote 1 Thessalonians. Caesar had come back to visit the city, and those who read Paul's letter knew that the word for Caesar's return was *parousia*.

That is the word Paul used when he wrote about the Lord coming down from heaven. It is the word that referred to a time when Caesar had given the citizens resources and then had visited to check on the rebuilding process. At that time, the people had met him outside the city, with all the pageantry of an imperial parade. (The event had even been described with the hyperbole of meeting Caesar in the clouds and with trumpets.) The people had escorted the emperor back inside the city to show him what they had done with the resources sent to them.

This is one reason Paul mentioned work and its importance. God would return one day, very much like Caesar had done, to see what the people had done with what He had invested in them.

QUILTING FOR THE KINGDOM OF GOD

A few years ago I (Jonathan) was hanging out with some quilting ladies at the church where I worked. Every week, a couple of dozen ladies made warm bedcovers for the underprivileged. They give their quilts to orphans, people with mental handicaps, kids in cancer wards, basically anyone who needed to keep warm. I listened to their stories, and I told them, "What you do now matters forever, so the picture you have in front of you when you think about forever matters right now. Your view of tomorrow determines how you live today.

In 1 Corinthians 15, Paul wrote at length about the resurrection. He spent fifty-eight verses making sure his listeners understood that the Christian idea of the resurrection of the body and the resurrection of creation differs greatly from the Greek idea of the immortality of the soul. But he ended that passage in a strange way:

> Therefore, my dear brothers and sisters, stand firm. Let nothing
> move you. Always give yourselves fully to the work of the Lord,
> because you know that your labor in the Lord is not in vain.
> (1 Corinthians 15:58)

He wanted Christians to know that their labor in the Lord is not in vain. In doing so, Paul indicated that the resurrection serves as motivation for what we do in this life.

Which brings us to one of the more bizarre passages in the Bible. It's also in 1 Corinthians, a few chapters before Paul wrote about the resurrection. This chapter makes some Christians nervous because it sort of sounds like a reference to purgatory.

> By the grace God has given me, I laid a foundation as a wise builder, and someone else is building on it. But each one should build with care. For no one can lay any foundation other than the one already laid, which is Jesus Christ. If anyone builds on this foundation using gold, silver, costly stones, wood, hay or straw, their work will be shown for what it is, because the Day will bring it to light. It will be revealed with fire, and the fire will test the quality of each person's work. If what has been built survives, the builder will receive a reward. If it is burned up, the builder will suffer loss but yet will be saved—even though only as one escaping through the flames. (1 Corinthians 3:10–15)

What we do with our life will be judged, and everything that is in line with what God is trying to do will be revealed. The rest will be burned. In this book, the two of us have tried to clear up the confusion that has led Christians to believe that God's ultimate plan is to burn the world. We believe Christians have largely misunderstood God's judgment.

The flames of God's judgment refine and restore God's creation, but they don't destroy it. What we do now that is in harmony with the world God created will be restored and will last forever. The things we have done that are not in harmony with God's intentions will be singed away.

Failure is not the worst thing that can happen to any of us. The worst thing is to succeed at something that doesn't matter. But Paul seemed to be saying, "Take heart. Far more matters (including matter) than you know."

When the day of the Lord comes, it will reveal what you did with your life.

The things we do that align with God's desires and His new creation will last.

N. T. Wright put it like this:

Every minute spent teaching a severely handicapped child to read or to walk; every act of care and nurture, of comfort and support, for one's fellow human beings and for that matter one's fellow nonhuman creatures; and of course every prayer, all Spirit-led teaching, every deed that spreads the gospel, builds up the church, embraces and embodies holiness rather than corruption, and makes the name of Jesus honored in the world—all of this will find its way, through the resurrecting power of God, into the new creation that God will one day make.[3]

In the words of C. S. Lewis, "No good thing is destroyed." Which means that the church and every Christian are called to live and work in this world that is being made new by God even now!

It is a new kind of life, a new kind of work in the world, that is powered by the resurrection of the Son of God and the hope for the resurrection of the entire universe. The resurrection is the ultimate vision for new life, and the ultimate call for us not to waste this one.

We wanted to write this book because we believe that what people hope toward is what people will live for. Hope is in short supply, which helps explain why there is such a disconnect between what we say we believe and how we live.

When the Bible talks about Jesus's call for us to live differently, it's not so you can earn more of God's grace. The reason you are called to live so differently than everyone else is because you are going to be part of the new heaven and the new earth, where everything will be turned upside down.

We are called to live in a way that shows the world an alternate reality as we are prepared for that reality right now.

In the ancient world, people cared little for how they treated one another. It was commonly assumed that the gods were indifferent, so there was a saying, "As above, so below." But Jesus-followers reversed that, because Jesus did care.[4] What we do here can matter forever! That is why what we think about heaven matters so much.

If we think God's future has nothing to do with our lives and this world, then it won't affect how we live. It's possible to be a Christian and waste your life. It's possible to think that the gospel is all about another time and another place, and totally miss out on what God is doing right in front of you.

HOPE IS WORKING

Martin Luther King Jr. famously wrote about this from a jail in Birmingham, Alabama. He pointed out that the white church leaders promised oppressed African Americans pie in the sky after they died, but white church leaders did nothing to help set the world right in this life. He said it this way:

> I have watched many churches commit themselves to a completely otherworldly religion which makes a strange, un-Biblical distinction between body and soul, between the sacred and the secular.[5]

These days it seems that Christians have to choose between what Dallas Willard referred to as more than one gospel having to do with "sin management."[6] One gospel recognizes that the world is broken and that evil systems oppress people. But it often doesn't deal with the evil in each one of us. It doesn't help us deal with evil on a personal level.

The other gospel knows there is sin in each of us and we each need Jesus to save us from ourselves. But it doesn't deal with the injustices in the world. Salvation becomes seen as an individual thing, for personal piety and not to bring God's justice to bear on earthly injustice.

But the gospel that Jesus preached did both. It was called the Kingdom of God, and it refused to separate the physical from the spiritual. Instead, it brought together heaven and earth and the welfare of people's souls with the need to fight injustice, which plagues the bodies of the people whose souls need to be saved.

Your work is important, not just so you can contribute money to a church or a ministry, but because you get to partner with God. You get to contribute to the healing of the world. If you are a follower of Jesus, that is your vocation.

Whenever I sit next to someone on a commercial flight, the person almost invariably asks, "What do you do?" When I say, "I'm a preacher," I almost always follow it with, "I believe that in the sixties and seventies people looked back on the church and said, 'How could we have been so racist?' In the nineties and 2000s, we looked back and said, 'How could we have been so patriarchal?' I think now we are starting to look back and say, 'How could we have been so selfish?'"

Then I add, "All across the country people are starting to wake up to the reality that the church is called to be a compelling force for good in *this world,* not the next."

We believe church matters, not because it's the only place to meet God, but because it's where we learn to meet God everywhere we find ourselves outside the church. Our job is not to just hold on until we die and go to heaven. We have work to do on earth.

Since the resurrection, Christians have understood that God hasn't given up on this world. But that vision, the one you have for your life in this world, is not in vain. It is from God.

THERE IS A TREE

In his book *Every Good Endeavor,* Tim Keller tells about how *The Lord of the Rings* came to be written.[7]

J. R. R. Tolkien had worked on the material for *The Lord of the Rings* for years when he realized he was getting old. He had spent decades working on this epic story, and he hadn't yet written a page. Instead, he had created entire worlds and cultures and languages. He wanted the eventual story to have a universe to live in.

Then he realized he had been so obsessed with the details that he had not been writing the story. He wondered if he would die before he could complete his dream of writing the epic novels we know today.

You probably know that Tolkien finished his book. But before he sat down to write it, he wrote a short story, "Leaf by Niggle." It's about a man named Niggle whose life mission is to make a painting of a tree.

Niggle is an English word meaning someone "obsessed with the details." While Niggle really wants to paint the tree, he keeps obsessing over the first couple of leaves. He is committed to getting the leaves done perfectly. But Niggle is old.

People keep asking him to help them. It dawns on Niggle that he may not be able to finish his dream of painting the tree. He works on it, but sure enough he dies before he finishes.

It doesn't take Sigmund Freud to know that Tolkien was writing about his own life. He wrote the story right after it dawned on him that he might not live to create his own masterpiece. He told us about the anxiety of his own work by telling us a story.

When they find Niggle dead at home, someone notices the partially finished painting. It was a basic sketch of a tree, with one leaf intact. But the leaf is exquisite, so they put the painting in a museum. For a while people come to see it. A few were impressed by the incredible detail, but most just saw an unfinished painting. Niggle's life work blessed a few people and ultimately was forgotten.

But . . . the story does not end there.

Niggle went to heaven and the first thing he saw was the Tree. *His tree!*

Our work can be frustrating. There are days where we feel like we're just painting the same leaf again. But in our better days, we know that all of our work matters more than we could ever imagine. There is a new day coming that won't be like the previous ones.

A world is breaking into this one that is full of the glory of God, and in that world there will be no more suffering or pain. I will paint the leaves of my life as well as possible, because I believe in the best parts of my heart that there is a Tree.

That is the Christian hope. It is a vision for a future that impacts every part of our now. So take heart, plumbers and musicians. Take heart, teachers and doctors. Take heart, electricians and carpenters.

Take heart, church. Your labor is in the Lord . . . and your work is not in vain! There is a Tree, and your hope is working.

Acknowledgments

We write this book from a deep love for God and a conviction that what happens in this world matters to Him. We believe the resurrection of Jesus has made restoration available to the entire world, and we are eager to share the good news that flows from the empty tomb.

Our two churches—the Highland Church and the Sycamore View Church—have been so gracious and supportive. The journey of restoration we have been on with our church families has provided so much of the content and inspiration for this book. Serving you is more than a job to us. It is an honor to share life with you.

There were a lot of late-night and early-morning writing sessions. We would like to thank Diet Dr. Pepper, lattes, coffee with hazelnut cream, and the energy drinks we have devoured while staying up late to write. We hope that each sip has been worth it.

God's love for cities has taught us to engage Abilene and Memphis with hope. The restoration of God has led us to renounce cynicism and doubt, because we don't have time for either. Joy and hope are better ways to live. We love our cities, and we believe the best days for us are ahead of us, not behind us.

To our agent, Wes Yoder, thank you for believing in two young pastors. We could not have made it this far without you.

To the WaterBrook publishing team, thank you for believing in this book. You pushed us hard, and you made the writing process life-giving and full of joy. To Ron Lee, our editor, you have been a true partner throughout this process. Thank you.

To our children: Eden, Samuel, Hannah, and Joel Storment, and

Truitt and Noah Ross, we want to raise you with gospel imagination, believing that you have something beautiful to offer to the world.

And to our wives, Leslie and Kayci, how can we thank you for your love, support, and encouragement? You have taught us that marriage is to be a witness to the world of God's grace, power, and restoration. You deserve a trip to the beach, and we promise to make that happen sometime soon.

Discussion Questions

The Effect of Heaven on Earth Today

Using just fourteen words, Jesus taught us how to pray *and* how to live. "Your kingdom come, your will be done, on earth as it is in heaven" (Matthew 6:10). God's Kingdom is in evidence when God's will is lived out on earth. That's how we can bring the life of God to the people around us. Or, in the words of Jonathan Storment and Josh Ross, we can bring heaven to earth.

For Discussion

Use this guide to spark conversations with a friend, or in a group discussion, to explore further the idea that the life of heaven can be brought to earth. For openers:

1. When you think of heaven, what is the first thing that comes to mind?
2. How do you respond to the view that God's Kingdom involves carrying out God's will on earth, and thus bringing the ways of heaven to those around you?
3. Consider this statement by the authors, then discuss your reactions: "It's possible to think that the gospel is all about another time and another place, and totally miss out on what God is doing right in front of you."

Introduction: Good News for a Change

1. The authors revisit the story of Cornelius, a Roman centurion who received a vision from God (see Acts 10:3–4). The following day, Peter also had a vision (see Acts 10:11–16). Peter then went to the home of Cornelius, in violation of religious rules prohibiting contact between a Jew and a Gentile (see Acts 10:28–46). The authors point out that two leading characters in this story got saved. One was a Gentile and a Roman, the other a Jew and a leading follower of Jesus. How do you respond to the idea that a follower of Jesus can still be converted?

2. The authors write that Peter "experiences a deeper conversion into the mission of Jesus." Would you agree that learning more about what Jesus desires of us can be the equivalent of another conversion? Why or why not?

3. In what ways do you think Christians still need to be converted?

4. God used an ethnic and religious outcast, the Gentile Cornelius, to give Peter and other followers of Jesus a clearer understanding of God's work. What have you learned personally from unbelievers?

Chapter 1: When Heaven Comes Home

1. The authors revisit the story of Cornelius, a Roman centurion who received a vision from God (see Acts 10:3–4). The following day, Peter also had a vision (see Acts 10:11–16). Peter then went to the home of Cornelius, in violation of religious rules prohibiting contact between a Jew and a Gentile (see Acts 10:28–46). The authors point out that two leading characters in this story got saved. One was a Gentile and a Roman, the other a Jew and a leading follower of Jesus. How do you respond to the idea that a follower of Jesus can still be converted?

2. The authors write that Peter was "converted deeper into the mission of Jesus." Would you agree that learning more about what Jesus desires of us can be the equivalent of another conversion? Why or why not?

3. In what ways do you think Christians still need to be converted?

4. God used an ethnic and religious outcast, the Gentile Cornelius, to give Peter and other followers of Jesus a clearer understanding of God's work. What have you learned personally from unbelievers?

Chapter 2: When the Saints Go Marching ~~In~~ Out

1. When you read the Bible, do you see the world as something a Christian should retreat from or run into?

2. The Bible says to "flee the evil desires of youth" (2 Timothy 2:22) and to "abstain from all appearance of evil" (1 Thessalonians 5:22, KJV). Should Christians maintain a distance from people and situations that are not God honoring? Why or why not?

3. Jesus called us to be salt and light (see Matthew 5:13 regarding salt, and Acts 13:47 regarding light). The authors write: "Each week greets us with moments to march into places of injustice and extreme forms of pain, sometimes to heal and cure it; other times to simply be present in the mess." Have you been involved in such situations? Discuss the situation and the outcome.

4. Heaven is free of violence, hunger, poverty, hatred, prejudice, deception, and greed. Does this list paint an accurate picture of what the Kingdom of God, if fully realized on earth, would look like? Why or why not?

Chapter 3: The Groans of Creation

1. Do you think of heaven as a far-off location, as a future reality, or as a present reality—or do you picture it in a different way? Discuss your understanding of heaven.
2. The Bible indicates that heaven is a realm in which everything is according to God's will. What would life on earth look like if every individual and every part of society operated on that basis?
3. Jesus said when one of His followers does anything for "one of the least of these brothers and sisters of mine," the person is performing the same act of kindness, assistance, or mercy to Jesus directly (see Matthew 25:40). Jesus is present in the person who ministers to others as well as in those who receive help. Have you ever had a sense of this when you entered the world of another person? Talk about it.

Chapter 4: Heaven Is Not the End of the World

1. *Los Angeles Times* journalist Joel Stein has written that the way Christians most often talk about heaven makes it appear to be less real than earth. Do you agree? Why or why not?
2. Is there a danger in giving the impression that heaven is a far-off, spiritual realm reserved for God, angels, and departed saints? Discuss.
3. Jesus described God's Kingdom—sometimes referring to it as the kingdom of heaven—in surprisingly ordinary terms. He said it is like a mustard seed and yeast (see Luke 13:18–21). Jesus also compared God's Kingdom to treasure hidden in a field, to a merchant looking for pearls, and to fishermen pulling in a net filled with fish (see Matthew 13:44–48). How do you respond to the idea that heaven is more like earth than many of us suspect?

Chapter 5: The Flames of Heaven

1. Christians have been accused of being too concerned about who's "in" and who's "out" when it comes to following Jesus. Do you feel such criticism is justified? Why or why not?

2. Jesus addressed this issue in a parable about sheep and goats. At issue is people's perceptions of their relationship with the Lord. But the Lord didn't agree with them in all cases. Read the parable and discuss its implications (see Matthew 25:31–46).

3. Some of us will be surprised when we meet the Lord face-to-face—realizing that we are not the sheep or goat we thought we were. What would you say is the primary point of the parable (see Matthew 25:31–46)? How would you define "sheep" and "goat" as those terms apply to who is part of God's Kingdom?

4. The authors write: "There are things that matter and things that don't," in reference to how we live and what we live for. They suggest we ask ourselves hard questions about how we use our money, our time, and our influence. How do you respond to their suggested approach to a self-inventory?

Chapter 6: A Marriage Made in Heaven

1. Jesus liked to party as much as anyone. Religious leaders frequently condemned His tendency to eat and drink and spend time with "sinners." How would you translate Jesus's love of celebration into a Kingdom practice today?

2. Jesus compared heaven to a wedding banquet. However, the authors write: "If you were to stop someone on the street and ask her what she thought heaven was like, I doubt she would say, 'It's a lot like a wedding'" (see Matthew 22:1–9). Does feasting at a banquet or celebrating a wedding open your eyes to a deeper understanding of heaven? If so, how?

3. In referring to the Kingdom of God, Jesus told about a wedding parade. A groom was so madly in love that he showed up at midnight, a highly unusual time to begin a wedding parade (see Matthew 25:1–13). Have you ever felt that God's love speeds His response to your needs and to the needs of others? Discuss.

Chapter 7: Guilty Parties

1. Perhaps the most-frequently repeated parable of Jesus is the story of the prodigal son (see Luke 15:11–32). The father has been keeping a lookout for his son who was lost. What is your first thought about a God who keeps checking for a person's return? What does that indicate about the Father's heart?

2. As soon as the son was in sight, the father ran to embrace him. Then the father escorted the wayward son to a party in his honor. According to an earthly view of fairness, what is wrong in this scene?

3. Meanwhile, the obedient older son complained that his rebellious brother had been given a free pass. With whom do you side, the older son who had served faithfully or the irresponsible son who wasted his inheritance? Discuss your response.

4. The older son told his father, "All these years I've been slaving for you . . ." (Luke 15:29). He viewed his relationship to his father as slavery. In what ways do you see a similar attitude among Christians?

Chapter 8: A Symphony of Grace

1. The parable of the prodigal son is so rich it warrants further consideration. The authors point out that the younger brother had broken every commandment except possibly the prohibition against adultery. "And that," they write, "was only because, to our knowl-

edge, he had never married." If any other person's life has been more wasted than this, what would it look like?

2. We know that the younger brother did one thing right: he came home. His father welcomed him, no questions asked. What does that type of love say to you?

3. The older brother, according to the authors, was blind to one major flaw: pride. How do you see pride at work among Christians today?

4. The older brother would likely have required the younger brother to undergo a public confession, a detailed expression of heartfelt apology, and possibly a period of proving himself before a party was held. But the father started preparations for a feast right away. What types of requirements do you see Christians placing on those they feel have lived outside of God's teaching?

Chapter 9: Jesus Throws the Best Parties

1. Josh Ross's former church hosted an outreach event—a barbecue held on the church grounds. But none of the neighbors attended. When the congregation moved the next barbecue to the courtyard of a nearby apartment complex, a large number of neighbors showed up. Why do you think Christians often expect outreach efforts to succeed when they are held on church grounds?

2. Josh writes: "The more we looked at Jesus, the more we were convinced that the church often is at its best when it gives up home-field advantage." What are your thoughts on his observation?

3. Church members were told in advance that if they planned to socialize only with fellow church members at the barbecue, then they should not attend. Are you surprised such a rule was enforced? Why or why not?

4. Can you think of ways the church has emphasized making life "safer" even if it might inhibit ministry? Discuss your observations.

Chapter 10: A Party Waiting to Happen

1. The authors write about the exchange between Jesus and the criminal hanging on a cross beside Him. In a situation that likely was hopeless in the eyes of the criminal, Jesus turned everything around. When have you seen a seemingly hopeless situation turned into the miracle of restoration?

2. The authors mention the condemned criminal as an example of a person who didn't try to dress up his sin. They write: "There is no need to try to trick [God] or pretend to be something you're not." When are you tempted to try to minimize your neediness before God?

3. There is no record in Scripture that the condemned criminal had listened to a gospel presentation. He simply acknowledged his need and asked for help (see Luke 23:40–43). Jesus responded immediately, welcoming the man into Paradise. What would be applications of this in the church today?

4. According to the authors, "Jesus . . . sees that we are approaching, even if we're doing so with doubts or shame—even if we fear that He will turn away from us." How do you respond to the view that faith need not be unshakeable before a person will receive a response from God?

Chapter 11: Your Blessed Life Now

1. Tony Campolo is a well-known Christian author and speaker. The authors recall a speech in which Dr. Campolo suggested that to describe many American churches, you could simply reverse the Beatitudes (see Matthew 5:3–12). What do you think of his critique?

2. By human standards, Jesus could be seen as blessing all the wrong people (see Matthew 5:3–12). How do you respond to this observation?

3. The authors write: "Try to live in the power of the words [of the Beatitudes] for a week." Have you ever tried such an experiment? What happened? If not, what would you expect to be the outcome?

4. The authors suggest that Jesus was crucified for living out His teaching that "God's blessing belongs to the least of these," in direct opposition to the social and political systems of His day. When have you seen faithfulness to Jesus's way of life result in penalties from society?

Chapter 12: It's About Time

1. Christians traditionally have talked about the hope of salvation, which links hope to the afterlife. What are your thoughts regarding the importance of hope in everyday life on earth?

2. A seventy-year-old Texan named Arnold was working on his ranch when Lil, his wife, rushed out to tell him she had been diagnosed with stage four cancer. For two more years, writes Jonathan Storment, "I saw a man love a woman fully . . . And then finally and cruelly, cancer took Lil from Arnold." Arnold now waits with great loss but also with hope. What do you see as the connection between loss and hope?

3. The authors write: "The promise of Scripture is that one day all things will be restored." They quote Isaiah: "Never again will there be in it an infant who lives but a few days, or an old man who does not live out his years; the one who dies at a hundred will be thought a mere child; the one who fails to reach a hundred will be considered accursed. They will build houses and dwell in them; they will plant vineyards and eat their fruit" (Isaiah 65:20–21). Discuss the idea that God will restore all things, replacing grief with hope.

Chapter 13: How to Lose the Fear of Failure

1. It's not unusual for people to congregate with others who are like them. When this results in Christians separating themselves from those who hold differing beliefs, what is often the outcome?

2. Some Christians set up parallel structures that segregate Christians from the wider society in education, recreation, community involvement, and other areas. How do you feel about these parallel structures for Christians?

3. Does involvement in Christian activities ever prevent you from having time to engage with those outside the church? What would be lost if you remained involved in the same types of activities, but did them with nonchurch friends?

4. Fear can easily become something that influences us. We see it in news reports, political campaigns, entertainment, and even apocalyptic religious teachings. How do you guard against the negative influence of fear?

Chapter 14: What Comes Next?

1. The authors maintain that God's judgment does not mean that God will destroy the world, but rather that our lives will be exposed and judged. "Everything that is in line with what God is trying to do will be revealed," they write. How do you feel about God's judgment?

2. What does the new heaven and the new earth mean to you (see Revelation 21:1)?

3. What difference does it make in your life that Jesus connected the life of heaven to how God's people live on earth?

Notes

Introduction

1. Joshua Ryan Butler, *The Skeletons in God's Closet* (Nashville: Thomas Nelson, 2014), 7–8.

Chapter 1

1. Conversation between Oshea Israel and Mary Johnson, Story-Corps, http://storycorps.org/listen/mary-johnson-and-oshea-israel/. See also Dave Isay, "You Killed My Son and I Forgive You," *The Daily Beast,* October 23, 2013, www.thedailybeast.com/articles /2013/10/23/you-killed-my-son-and-i-forgive-you.html.

Chapter 2

1. This point is debated. We acknowledge that authorship and the target audience of Ephesians is often debated by well-known and respected scholars and theologians. In this chapter, we do not attempt to enter into a scholarly debate about either. Ephesus was a prominent city in the first-century world, and the New Testament has a lot to say about the city.
2. As you read Ephesians 5:18, bear in mind that the people of Ephesus who read or heard these words would receive them in the context of their pagan, sexualized society.
3. Anonymous, "When the Saints Go Marching In," 1896, public domain, www.soundclick.com/bands/_music_lyrics.cfm?bandid =431747&songID=9161449.

4. Sara Groves, "When the Saints," copyright © 2007 by INO Records, www.lyricsmode.com/lyrics/s/sara_groves/when_the _saints.html#!.

5. See Ronald Sider, *Rich Christians in an Age of Hunger* (Nashville: W Publishing Group, 1997), 107–8.

Chapter 3

1. Philip Yancey, *Rumors of Another World* (Grand Rapids, MI: Zondervan, 2003), 184.

2. Mark Buchanan, *Your God Is Too Safe* (Colorado Springs: Multnomah Books, 2001), 226–27.

3. William Willimon, *Peculiar Speech: Preaching to the Baptized* (Grand Rapids, MI: William B. Eerdmans Publishing Company, 2002), 90.

4. Barbara A. Holmes, *Joy Unspeakable* (Minneapolis: Augsburg Fortress, 2004), 70–73, 75.

5. For more on this, see Timothy Keller, *King's Cross* (New York: Dutton Publishing, 2011), 93.

Chapter 4

1. For the transcription of Supreme Court testimony, see *Abington School District v. Schempp* and *Murray v. Curlett* 374 U.S. 203 (1963).

2. As a side note, I have noticed that there is a correlation between the number of capital letters used in a sentence and the amount of crazy in the person writing the sentence.

3. Years later we found out that what Sim was really doing was saying, "In a few moments some guys are about to walk over here to hit on you. They weren't brave enough to approach you by themselves, so please just ignore them and walk away." Well played, Simran.

4. For a more detailed explanation of the evolution of how Americans have thought of the Christian afterlife, see Gary Scott Smith, *Heaven in the American Imagination* (New York: Oxford University Press, 2011).

5. Joel Stein, "A Little Bit of Heaven on Earth," December 21, 2007, http://articles.latimes.com/2007/dec/21/news/OE-STEIN21/.

6. Stanley Grenz, *What Christians Really Believe—and Why* (Louisville, KY: Westminster John Knox, 1998), 156.

7. For more on the Rwandan genocide, see a report prepared by the United Human Rights Council. Found at www.unitedhuman-rights.org/genocide/genocide_in_rwanda.htm/.

8. For more on this aspect of the Rwandan genocide, see Lee Camp, *Mere Discipleship* (Grand Rapids, MI: Baker Books, 2008), 19.

9. For more on this aspect of the Rwandan genocide, see Camp, *Mere Discipleship*, 20.

10. Dallas Willard, *The Divine Conspiracy* (New York: HarperCollins, 1998), 40.

11. See Isaiah 25:9–12; 65:17–25. These are passages that the New Testament—in particular Revelation 21–22—builds on.

12. Randy Alcorn makes the observation that a huge percentage of the biblical words of hope start with the prefix "re." See Randy Alcorn, *Heaven* (Wheaton, IL: Tyndale House Publishing, 2004), 88. This makes sense, because it means to return something to a condition before it was ruined or broken. See Albert Wolters, quoted in Alcorn, *Heaven*, 90.

13. We believe this reference refers to Jesus's return to take people home.

14. This observation came from Barbara Rossing, *The Rapture Exposed* (New York: Westview Press, 2004), 146.

15. To be fair, this gentleman apologized toward the end of his life and repented of how he'd stirred up so much hysteria.

Chapter 5

1. Dallas Willard, *The Divine Conspiracy* (New York: HarperCollins, 1998), 301.

2. Peter Scazzero, *Emotionally Healthy Spirituality* (Grand Rapids, MI: Zondervan, 2014), 30.

3. N. T. Wright, *Surprised by Hope* (New York: HarperCollins, 2008), 105, 121.

4. C. S. Lewis, *The Magician's Nephew,* The Chronicles of Narnia (San Francisco: Harper Collins, 2007), 147.

5. The question comes particularly from the New Testament letter of 2 Peter, which is talking about the common idea of the Day of the Lord. It's the classic Jewish idea, which the prophets talked about: the judgment of God. It was something that the people of God have always looked forward to. The word that Peter uses here is a form of the word *heúr ka*. It means "exposed" or "laid bare." (It's where we get the English word *eureka*.) The idea isn't that all the world will be destroyed, but rather found out. Remember the fire mentioned here isn't about destroying the entire world. Peter tells this story in the context of the story of Noah's flood. It was a flood that didn't destroy the world but judged it, refined it. Peter is saying, "Rest assured God is going to do something like that again" (see 2 Peter 3:13). The Day of the Lord doesn't mean the world will be destroyed but refined, and at that time our works will be exposed for what they are. This is why Peter says, "So what kind of people ought we to be?" When heaven comes down, when the Day of the Lord happens, what we've done will be exposed.

6. John Ortberg, *Christianity Today* online, May 8, 2013, www .christianitytoday.com/ct/2013/may-web-only/man-from-another -time-zone.html.

7. John Ortberg, *Soul Keeping* (Grand Rapids, MI: Zondervan, 2014), 193.

Chapter 6

1. In Ephesians 5, Paul calls marriage a profound mystery. In the Greek, he says this is a *mega mysterion*. This is why Paul ends his letter to the Ephesians by saying, "Pray also for me, that whenever I speak, words may be given me so that I will fearlessly make known the mystery of the gospel, for which I am an ambassador in chains" (6:19–20). What Paul is doing in his chains, he thinks Christian couples are doing in their marriages.

2. Douglas E. Neel and Joel A. Pugh, *The Food and Feasts of Jesus* (Lanham, MD: Rowan and Littlefield, 2012), 120.

3. Neel and Pugh, *Food and Feasts of Jesus,* 124.

4. This sheds some light on Jesus's response to the Pharisees about the rules of fasting and Sabbath being suspended for a wedding feast. For more on this, see Neel and Pugh, *Food and Feasts of Jesus,* 128.

5. N. T. Wright, *Surprised by Hope* (New York: HarperCollins, 2008), 105.

6. C. S. Lewis, *The Four Loves* (Orlando, FL: Harcourt, 1960), 114.

Part 2

1. A lot of people are interested in the so-called Gnostic gospels, the ones the early church didn't accept into the Bible. It seems like every time you turn on the History Channel there is another program about the forbidden "Gospel of Thomas." or Judas. We have this hunch that the church is holding out on us and not letting us see the full picture of Jesus. But if you ever read one of the "forbidden" gospels, you'd know that the

church really had an easy job of distinguishing them from the ones they accepted into the canon of Scripture. It's not that they show Jesus in a slightly different light; it's that the accounts found in these "gospels" are not remotely related to the Jesus of Nazareth. Here's how Francis Spufford wrote about it: "The Jesus of the orthodox story treats people with deep attention even when angry. Their Jesus zaps people with his divine superpowers if they irritate him. Orthodox Jesus says that everyone needs the love of God, and God loves everyone. Their Jesus has an inner circle you can be admitted to if you collect enough crisp packets. Orthodox Jesus likes wine, parties, and grilled fish for breakfast. Their Jesus thinks that human flesh and its appetites are icky." *Unapologetic* (New York: HarperCollins, 2013), 153–54.

Chapter 7

1. Dorothy Sayers, "The Other Six Deadly Sins," (Caxton Hall, Westminster, October 23, 1941), www.lectionarycentral.com /trinity07/Sayers.html.
2. Juliet Schor, *The Overworked American* (New York: BasicBooks, 1992), 170.
3. For more about this story, see John Blake, "'Most Hated,' Anti-Gay Preacher Once Fought for Civil Rights," May 14, 2010, www.cnn .com/2010/US/05/05/hate.preacher/.
4. Adelaide Pollard, "Have Thine Own Way," public domain.

Chapter 8

1. Mark Buchanan, *Your Church Is Too Safe* (Grand Rapids, MI: Zondervan, 2012), 132.

Chapter 9

1. G. K. Chesterton, *Orthodoxy* (New York: John Lane Company, 1908), 298–99.

Chapter 10

1. Placide Cappeau, "O Holy Night," 1847. Translated into English by John Sullivan Dwight, 1855, www.cyberhymnal.org/htm/o/h /oholynit.htm.
2. For more on this idea, see Philip Yancey, *What Good Is God?* (New York: FaithWords, 2010), 215–22.
3. For more on this, see Francis Spufford, *Unapologetic* (New York: HarperCollins, 2013), 7–9.
4. Louis C. K., "Louis C. K.'s Monologue," Saturday Night Live Transcripts, March 29, 2014, http://snltranscripts.jt.org/13 /13pmono.phtml/.
5. See John Lennon, "Imagine," 1971, www.youtube.com/watch?v =EJ72bYyEtBg/.
6. Spufford, *Unapologetic*, 12–13.

Chapter 11

1. See E. Randoph Richards and Brandon J. Brien, *Misreading Scripture with Western Eyes* (Downers Grove, IL: IVP Books, 2012), 75.
2. Pliny the Younger (Ep. 2.6), http://vroma.org/~hwalker/Pliny /Pliny02-06-E.html.
3. C. S. Lewis, *The Weight of Glory and Other Addresses* (New York: McMillan, 1949), 36–39.
4. Philip Yancey, *What Good Is God?* (New York: FaithWords, 2010), 75.

5. Sunday morning church bulletin from Our Lady of Lourdes Catholic Community, July 2012, www.huffingtonpost.com /2012/07/27our-lady-of-lourdes-catholic-community-bulletin _n_1710757.html.

Chapter 12

1. Little-known fact: this is the inspiration behind the song "Who Let the Dogs Out?"
2. For more on this, see Chris Huntington, "Learning to Measure Time in Love and Loss," *The New York Times,* December 26, 2013, www.nytimes.com/2013/12/29/fashion/learning-to-measure -time-in-love-and-loss.html?_r=0/.
3. For more on this, see the Work of the People interview with Brené Brown, www.theworkofthepeople.com/jesus-wept/.
4. Joni Eareckson Tada, "Joni's Story," 2–3, www.joniearecksontada story.com.

Chapter 13

1. "Specific Phobias," WebMD, www.webmd.com/anxiety-panic /specific- phobias?page=2.
2. "Fear/Phobia Statistics," Statistic Brain, www.statisticbrain.com /fear-phobia-statistics/.

Chapter 14

1. Note that when the prophets talk about the Age to Come, there almost always is a picture of an economy. An economy involves people working together. This is why in many biblical pictures of heaven we find a robust, thriving economy. We read about food and vineyards, wine, and people cooperating in groups to make it

happen. Heaven is the great celebration of God and God's creation, and parties take a lot of work.

2. We have written about this in greater detail in a previous chapter. But just as a reminder, this theology has more in common with one of the first heresies the church faced, called Gnosticism. This set of false teachings held that God doesn't think this world matters. Gnosticism promotes a gospel without a body attached, which is a false gospel without hope.

3. N. T. Wright, *Surprised by Hope* (New York: HarperCollins, 2008), 208.

4. In Matthew 16:19, Jesus told Peter that what happens on earth changes heaven!

5. Martin Luther King Jr., "Letter from a Birmingham Jail," *A Christian Reader in Social Ethics from the Bible to the Present* (Minneapolis: Fortress Press, 2012), 354.

6. Gary Black, *The Theology of Dallas Willard* (Eugene, OR: Pickwick, 2013), 148.

7. For more on this, see Tim Keller, *Every Good Endeavor* (New York: Dutton, 2012), 24–28.